Lead Like a Girl

A Leader's Journey from Aspirations to Achievements

Lovell Casiero

Library of Congress Cataloging-in-Publication Data
Casiero, Lovell, 2023
Lead Like a Girl: A Leader's Journey from Aspirations to Achievements / Lovell Casiero
First Edition
ISBN: 979-8-9892004-0-5 (paperback) | 979-8-9892004-1-2 (ebook)
Library of Congress Control Number: 2023918240

Book cover and design by Frances Owen
Photographs by Angela Phillips, Frozen In Time Photography

Unless otherwise indicated, all Bible passages quoted in this book are from the New International Version (NIV).

Printed in the United States of America

Dedication

With deep appreciation and love, this book is dedicated to my husband, Lenny Casiero, who has always been my unwavering wellspring of inspiration and support.

In addition, I extend this dedication to the remarkable tribal daughters I've had the privilege of gathering on my life's extraordinary journey. While there are too many to individually mention, if you are among them, you understand the profound impact you've had on my life. I am deeply grateful for the trust you've placed in me to be a significant part of your professional endeavors, personal life, and family. Being your mentor is a privilege I cherish, and the meaningful role you have played in my life is something I hold dear – now and always.

Contents

Introduction

It is my belief that nothing in life ever finishes like you thought it would when you started. FLC Business Consulting is an excellent example of that. When I started the company in 2015, I had a vision for the work we would provide and the clientele we would serve. It wasn't long before I realized there would be a shift in the vision. The clientele was different than I expected, and the assignment types were also different. It was a slight change, but even a 1% variation in a flight path can significantly impact where you arrive, depending on the length of the journey.

I envisioned a company that would support third-party management companies with consulting services in the commercial strategy discipline of the hospitality industry. Instead, I was called upon by asset managers, investors, and owners to audit the performance of third-party management companies or provide due diligence for their acquisitions. Our sales and marketing consulting expertise also serviced small businesses in the wellness, legal, and real estate industries. The services we offer have continued to evolve, and today, we also provide life and professional coaching for individuals who want to improve their status quo and achieve their goals.

I never dreamed FLC Business Consulting would also provide the publishing and marketing platform for my first book, but here we are. True to my first statement, the book has not finished like I thought it would when I had the vision and started writing. Based on the title, I expected to provide the reader with leadership lessons, and I assumed that my audience would be female. However, as I began to write, there were many epiphanies along the way.

First, I could not talk about the leadership lessons I have learned without including the life lessons I have learned. Therefore, I realized I would need to get up close and personal with the reader, which meant being willing to share my personal life stories. One of my strongest beliefs about being a great leader is that you must be authentic. To be personally accountable to that belief meant I had to not only share the successes but also include the failures and opportunities.

When I committed to being all in with the good, the bad, and the ugly version of me, I realized that life lessons shaped the success of the leadership lessons I would share in this book. On any given day, they intermingle to achieve the results needed. Life lessons can provide solutions to leadership problems, and the same is true in the reverse. A good leader can apply leadership best practices to offer solutions to personal problems.

I hesitated for only a second when I decided to include my lessons of faith and the incredible heritage of ministry I come from. It wasn't originally something I thought I would do. So, if talking about my spiritual faith-based life will offend you, stop reading now, and I will refund your money.

My sister, April Raines, spoke at the Church of God world headquarters in Cleveland, Tennessee, for the service where our grandparents, Rev. A.B. and Gladys Whittington, were inducted into the Hall of the Prophets for their lifetime of work within this organization. April talked about our Christian heritage and our family's work in ministry. She spoke about what gets us up in the morning and gives us the resilience and the ability to power through no matter what the day brings. She said, "It is in our DNA; determination needed ahead, and that comes from our faith in God." I had never heard anyone put it that way, but I have never forgotten what she said, and I am a walking testimony that she is one hundred percent right.

I have not always made the best decisions. On any given day, the decisions you make are paving the way for your future. I am grateful for the grace I received even in times of poor judgment, and I hope that by sharing my story, you will realize you are never too far from the goal to achieve your dreams and visions. You can recover from the past and move forward from your present because the future is a blank page waiting to be written.

My second epiphany is that this book is not just for women. Don't let the title fool you. It is a book for leaders. It is not about gender; it is just told from a woman's voice. This book's life and leadership lessons are for men and women alike. If I have but one wish, I wish that whoever the reader is, they leave these pages a better version of themselves than when they started reading.

If you are a man considering reading this book, I highly recommend you do. You may gain some insight on how to work alongside women in a more collaborative and unified way. You may learn how to mentor the women on your team in a more meaningful way and how to best use the attributes they bring for the greater good of the team. Finally, if you have daughters, nieces, granddaughters, or just a woman in your life who you care deeply about and want to see her achieve her dreams, you may discover a new way to support and encourage her along the journey.

The other part of this book that did not turn out exactly like I thought it would pertains to the interviews of the amazing women who agreed to share their stories. My first list of potential interviews consisted only of women at the pinnacle of their career journey. I envisioned an interview where the interviewees would share a story supporting the previous chapter's lessons. Instead, I pivoted from a list made up only of females at the top and started including women at different places in their journey. These stories are personally my favorite part of the book. The heart and soul of each story and the passion of these women come to life in their pages. I also did not expect so many of the lessons in this book to come from them and not me as the author. When that started to happen, it was magic. I learned something from every one of them, and I am so excited to introduce them to you.

I also realized every human has a unique and interesting story. It has been said that everyone has skeletons, but I hope and pray that what you find in the pages of this book are the blessings weaved into everyone's stories. The kind of blessings that come from the people they surround themselves with, the opportunities where they say "yes" to giving back or paying it forward, and most importantly, the gratitude they have for the life they were given. Every person has the potential to embody good and evil, and on any given day, one side or the other can show up. I hope you will find tools and resources in these pages that will help you control the evil and expound on the good to show up each day a better version of you than before.

At the end of each chapter, there are eight takeaways; I chose to have this number because eight is the number of new beginnings. It is my desire that *Lead Like a Girl* will help you validate your attributes as a leader and identify opportunities for new beginnings.

As you read this book, you will begin to realize you are in control of how you define each new day. With that in mind, I have provided a blank page following each chapter for you to reflect on what you've read. Think of it as a clean slate for you to consider how the lessons can help you outline the path to achieving your vision of your true purpose. I wish you much courage and grace as you continue your journey to greatness.

Writing this book has reminded me of how blessed my life has been, and I am so grateful you have decided to read my story. I hope you will enjoy my journey from aspirations to achievements and that at the end, I will have shared something that will help you find your purpose and achieve your dreams. More than anything, I hope to have been a blessing to you.

Psalms 51:10 – Create in me a pure heart, Oh God, and renew a steadfast spirit within me.

CHAPTER ONE

Shaping Belief Systems

Lessons from Strong Women

F rom the time we are little girls, we are conditioned by the influences of our families and especially the women who raised
us. Quite often, from generation to generation, the struggles of
women in business and leadership are passed from one generation
to another.

When I was a little girl, I always loved family gatherings. My
paternal grandmother, Gladys Whittington, was a pastor's wife
and the mother of ten children. I do not believe she ever worked
a job or earned a paycheck; however, she was one of the hard-
est-working women I ever knew. At family holiday gatherings, she
would cook and prepare the meal for days until the day of the
event. Without fail, when the buffet was ready and the blessing was
said, my grandmother would say to the other females and children,
"Let the men go first." I always believed everyone should have
stood back and let her go first instead. After all, she did most of the
work to ensure everyone had a good meal and family fellowship,
and there was no doubt she would stay in the kitchen until the last
dish was washed. However, that wasn't how my grandmother was
raised; she was taught from an early age to serve the men in her life,
and in her mind, that was the right way to do it.

My maternal grandmother, Ada Gasaway, was also an interesting woman. Her mother died when she was a newlywed of just a
few months. She was the oldest of six, and her baby brother was

only two months old at the time of her mother's passing. Her father, a mill worker, was faced with raising five children and felt the only option was to place them in foster care. Grandmother would tell the story of how she went to the "big boss man" at the mill and pleaded with him to give her a supervisor's house instead of the house they provided for young couples. She must have been very convincing because they gave her the larger house, and she brought her siblings to live with her and kept them together. I do not know if she had any personal dreams or goals of being more than a mill worker. When she decided to put her life aside and keep her family together in some way, big or small, it changed the course of her life forever.

When my grandmother Gasaway was in her 80th year, I asked her what she would tell me and what wisdom she would impart. She said, "Lovell, always remember you are not better than anyone else, and no one is better than you."

My mother grew up in a multi-generational household made up mostly of men. I have never heard her say anything negative about her life growing up. In fact, she only tells fond stories of those years, and at the end of each one, she usually says, "I had a good childhood." My mother is a very strong woman, and she has been my rock of Gibraltar for as long as I can remember. I can't help wondering: as good as her childhood was, did the circumstances create the strength I know in her? It must have been interesting being raised in a male-dominated household. Her uncles probably spoiled her, but at the same time, they were her role models, and she saw strength in them. I can also imagine that there were times she had to act out to be noticed. I imagine they were very protective, and as she grew through her adolescent years, she had to stand up for herself.

This upbringing likely came in handy when, at 18 years old, she married my father. There were signs of trouble early in the marriage. Mom had no problem standing up for herself, however. She did not take the route of a victim but used the skills she learned growing up and stood up for herself, acting out if the situation called for it and, most importantly, never cowering down.

At 28 years old, she became a single mom to her seven-year-old and five-year-old daughters. While dealing with the hurt and betrayal of her ten-year marriage ending in divorce, she placed her needs on the back burner to care for her girls. At one time, I think she was working four jobs to make ends meet. I know she wanted a different path in her life, but instead, she sacrificed her dreams to provide for my sister Joy and me. However, deep down inside, that young girl inside her knew that just because you were born a woman did not mean you could not accomplish anything you set your mind to. She instilled that in me and Joy. As I start a new challenge, I often hear my mother say, "You can do anything you set your mind to."

When I married my husband Lenny Casiero in 1988, I was also blessed with a wonderful mother-in-law, Angela Casiero. Her life and career journey are one to take note of. The daughter of Italian immigrants, she was the oldest of four. I am certain she grew up in the kitchen of her childhood home because the woman could cook like no one I have ever met. The first time I met her, I was invited to Sunday dinner at her house. In those days, Italian sons did not bring just anyone to Sunday dinner. In April 1988, my daughter and I were honored to be her guests. That was the day I met the boss of all bosses, my mother-in-law, for the next 35 years.

She married Anthony B. Casiero in 1944 and, by the age of 34, was the mother of three sons. In 1970, her husband had a stroke and never fully recovered from the stroke. This became mom's life pivot. At the time, Lenny's dad owned a bar and restaurant, and his mom worked at the high school cafeteria serving the students of the community.

Her day-to-day life for the next five years was getting her husband up, feeding him breakfast, and placing him in his wheelchair in front of the television. She would go to work and serve the students, come home, and serve him lunch. She then returned to her job and later came home to prepare dinner for her sons.

Mom's career with the school system eventually led her to become the dietitian for the Highland, New York school system, serving the community's elementary, middle, and high schools. Many years later, when visiting her in the nursing home, I mentioned her career and referenced her title as a dietitian. She corrected me and said that wasn't really her title. Even though she was working as a dietician, she did not have a degree and, therefore, did not have the title. That said, she had a legacy, and many generations of Highland High School graduates will forever remember her culinary skills that made a school lunch taste like a home-cooked meal.

Side note: my father-in-law, whom I never had the pleasure of meeting, was in the hospitality industry, and in 1946, he held the position of managing director at the Hotel Wellington in New York City. I always imagined I was the daughter he never had, and he would have been so proud of my work in the hospitality industry. Mom always said, "He would have loved you." A conversation with Anthony B. Casiero is one of the first conversations I will seek out when I get to heaven.

Remembering my mother-in-law reminds me of the value of perseverance. She had no choice during those five years; she could not quit. Her husband and three sons were depending on her. She held that family together in the worst of times. She went on to be the only parent of three sons who found their way back home many times throughout their lives as they faced life's challenges.

She taught me the value of managing your finances; coming up in the era of the Great Depression, she was very frugal. Everything had a value; if she did not feel the price aligned with the true value, she could do without it. She also never stopped moving and never stopped using her mind. Two months before she would have celebrated her 101st birthday, she passed away. However, she was still calling the shots and was mentally sound. She was a solid example of grit and grace and always seemed to know which one the circumstances called for.

It is between the ages of 0 and 8 years old that are crucial years in child development. Life experiences can have profound and lasting effects. A child has developed the most important sensory and perception systems by kindergarten. Over the next several years, additional cognitive functions develop. During these years of development, the blueprint for decision-making, information retention, and emotional management shapes a person's social and emotional development.[1]

Your environment during these formative childhood years impacts your knowledge of what acceptable and unacceptable behavior as an adult is. You are also learning to be a good listener, persist through learning challenges, and control your emotions.

Everyone is plagued with conflicting belief systems at some time in their life; most of the time, it starts very early. There are many positive things I take away from my grandmothers and mother, but from the eyes of a child, it was very conflicting. "Let the men go first;" a newlywed willing to take on the challenge of raising a large family, instead of the life she must have imagined when she said, "I do."

Through these women, I learned an incredible work ethic. I learned to take care of my family. I believe I am made up of all the strength I saw in each of them. The sacrifices each of them made helped me develop a strong sense of love and compassion for others. I am blessed to have known them; sharing their DNA is undoubtedly the best part of me.

I consider my learned belief system a success today, even though many junctures in my journey could have taken me down a different path if I had not been able to see the positive and weed out the negative. Mom's voice in my head saying, "You can do whatever you set your mind to," was precisely the opposite of how she lived her life. She did not achieve everything she wanted to achieve, and her sacrifices cost her the dreams she had for her own life. One grandmother depended on her husband and later her children for provisions and her livelihood. The other grandmother was independent and ran her household like a boss.

How has your belief system affected the career choices you have made? Were you supported growing up with positive reinforcement and examples of perseverance? Did you learn "I can" instead of "I can't?" If you did not have positive influences, have you carried this baggage into your adult life? If you have, then it has undoubtedly hurt your career advancement, decisions, and, ultimately, your success as a woman in leadership.

We have come a long way, baby! Especially from the days of my grandmothers and mother. We have so many more opportunities and reasons to be successful. If you are allowing the voices and influences of the past to affect you negatively, you must recognize them and determine how you will develop new habits that will change your thoughts and actions. Thoughts are the hardest of the two to change. It is a mindset change that has been allowed to grow for many years, and to move away from these thought patterns that result in the actions, you must be willing to attack years of perverted thinking, learned behavior, and insecurities. It will not be easy, but it is never too late to try.

I encourage you to walk down memory lane; if you left too much of the positive and embraced the negative, start rewriting your story today.

TAKEAWAYS

1. **The Influence of Maternal Figures**: The stories of my grandmothers Whittington and Gasaway teach us the profound impact maternal figures can have on shaping belief systems. From Gladys, we understand the entrenched cultural expectations of women's roles within the family and the selflessness often expected of them. Grandmother Gasaway's story highlights the strength and sacrifice required to keep a family together against the odds. Both women's experiences illustrate that the roles and beliefs instilled in us from a young age can profoundly affect our perceptions of duty, work ethic, and family responsibilities.

2. **Equity and Self-Worth**: Grandmother Gasaway's advice to "remember you are not better than anyone else, and no one is better than you" imparts a significant lesson on self-worth and equity. This teaches us that recognizing our inherent value is crucial and that humility coupled with confidence can guide us through life's challenges. This mindset is essential for young girls to develop a strong sense of self that is neither inflated nor diminished by comparison with others.

3. **Strength from Adversity**: My mother's upbringing in a male-dominated household and her subsequent challenges in marriage and as a single mother illustrate how strength is often forged in adversity. Her ability to stand up for herself and her children demonstrates the resilience that can develop when we are accustomed to asserting ourselves in difficult circumstances. It's an important lesson in the transformative power of challenges in developing personal fortitude.

4. **Sacrifice and Prioritization**: The story of my mother working multiple jobs to support her family exemplifies the theme of sacrifice. It demonstrates how women often prioritize the needs of their families over their own dreams and ambitions. This teaches us about the complex decisions women make and the silent resilience behind the choices that shape the lives of those they love.

5. **The Legacy of Perseverance and Frugality**: My mother-in-law's life teaches the importance of perseverance and financial wisdom. Her frugality, a remnant from growing up in the era of the Great Depression, and her ability to keep going despite life's adversities, offer a lesson in managing personal and family crises with grace and practicality.

6. **The Importance of Early Childhood**: The ages of 0 to 8 are critical in child development, where belief systems and behaviors are formed. The sensory, perception, and cognitive functions developed during these years become the foundation for later decision-making and emotional intelligence. It's crucial to be mindful of the environment children grow up in as it significantly impacts their future self-image and behavior.

7. **Reshaping Conflicting Belief Systems**: I've reflected on conflicting messages received in childhood, where actions and advice didn't always align. This inconsistency between what is said and what is done can confuse belief systems. Still, it also teaches the importance of critical thinking and personal agency in choosing which values to adopt and which to reject.

8. **Reevaluating and Rebuilding Belief Systems**: The final message encourages us to reassess our belief systems

and the influences that have shaped them. It reminds us that regardless of past influences, we have the power to rewrite our narratives and pursue success. By recognizing and changing thought patterns that hold us back, we can overcome inherited insecurities and behavioral patterns, highlighting the possibility and necessity of personal growth and empowerment.

In summary, this chapter emphasizes the significance of self-awareness, understanding our upbringing and its impact, recognizing our own worth, and the importance of reshaping limiting beliefs for personal and professional growth.

REFLECTIONS

"The question isn't who's going to let me; it's who's going to stop me."

Ayn Rand

CHAPTER TWO

The Decades That Built Me

Reflection is Good for the Soul

I f I could write a letter to my younger self, I would send it to the 30-year-old me. At that time in my life, my family was in crisis, and I was about to face one of the biggest challenges of my life. Thirty years later, those circumstances feel more like a dream than reality. I am certain that I am a better person because of the faith and perseverance that brought me through the storm and to the shore.

I would tell myself, "Define your work; do not let your work define you." Ultimately, your career is a means to the meaningful things in life: your health, family, and personal happiness and well-being. No one will remember your title when you're gone.

A couple more things: "Treat your family like your friends and your friends like family. Lead like a girl. Remember, the boys are not better than you; they are just wired differently than you. Transitions will be hard. You will be afraid, but do not give into fear because you miss opportunities if you don't try new things."

Finally, the most important piece of advice I ever received is what my grandmother told me 30 years ago. She said, "Always be yourself and remember you're not better than anyone, and no one is better than you." So, I would tell myself, "Find the authentic version of you and go with it. Never waiver because you are trying to be what others think you should be. Be kind to yourself, give yourself the same grace you give others, and embrace the uniqueness of you, Lovell."

The Decades That Built Me

When I reflect on the decades of my life, I find the compassion to give myself grace. We are truly our own worst critics on any given day. Reflection can help us to understand how our decisions shaped our lives; karma is real, and we never stop learning.

Twenties – 1982 - 1991

To say I put every grey hair in my mother's head by the time I was twenty would be an understatement. God love her; she was always there to help me pick up the pieces of my poor decisions. At 20 years old, I was the mother of a two-year-old daughter and would soon be ending my seven-year relationship with my first husband. The relationship shaped me in a lot of ways. When I finally decided to free myself from mental and physical abuse, I learned two valuable things. I learned responsibility for another human being. The decisions I would make going forward included a daughter, and those decisions would not only shape my future but hers as well. I also learned it is okay to stand up for yourself when people are hurting you emotionally or physically. It is not just OK; it is important that you do so.

New York, here I come! Paul was twenty-one years my senior and recently separated from a 20+ year marriage, but that did not stop me from packing my bags and moving to New York with my five-year-old daughter. Yet another bad decision, but somehow, something good always comes out of adversity. Putting distance between us and my daughter's father was probably necessary for me to get away from him. Most importantly, during these three years, I found the hospitality industry – or the industry found me. It was love at first sight! I loved the work; I was good at it, and I was planted where I could grow.

They say the "third time's the charm," and the decision to move to New York allowed me to meet Lenny Casiero, my husband of

35 years. When we married, Lenny came with a big Italian family, and for the first time in eight years, my daughter and I had a stable family life.

This decade taught me the value of family and that relationships are complex. When you are in a relationship, whether it be family, friends, or colleagues, you must remember entering a relationship with anyone brings many good things, but it can also bring baggage. The baggage people bring to the relationship can be very taxing, and it takes work to find common ground.

Thirties – 1992 - 2001

Of all the decisions I made in my twenties, one I did not make was to go to college. Fortunately for me, the hospitality industry rewards you for your hard work and effort. There would be times in my life when I would try to leave hotels and do something different, but I would always find my way back.

In February 1992, Lenny, my daughter Leigh, and I visited my family in North Carolina for a post-holiday visit. I look back on that visit and specifically one conversation I had with my dad; my life was about to change drastically. The next eight years would be the college education I never had. They would shape me, challenge me, almost break me, but I would come out on the other side, a survivor.

In 1992, my dad, an evangelist, had been in television for 15 years. He had been preaching for 31 years, and I was approaching my thirtieth birthday. Sitting at the kitchen table, he asked me if anything ever happened where he could not keep the ministry going, would I promise him that I would? I remember saying, "Yes, Daddy, I'll do whatever I can." What I know about that conversation today is that it was not simply a promise to my dad but a divine appointment. At the time, I did not even know I was saying yes to a calling that would rewrite my story.

In October 1992, I became the founder and president of the Christian Correspondence Church. I completed my first merger and acquisition when I took over the assets of my dad's ministry. My stepmother, Susan, and I liquidated assets from the previous organization to pay legal bills and relocated to our offices to Fayetteville, North Carolina. My dad was sentenced to 55 years in prison, and I had four siblings under the age of 20 still dependent on dad for support. The next decade would be the hardest of my life to date. I've always heard that what doesn't kill you makes you stronger. I am a living testimony of the truth in that statement. There were many challenges and accomplishments, and each one taught me more life, career, and relationship lessons than I can number. Several years after my dad's ministry was restored and back in his capable hands, he thanked me for what I did to keep the ministry going. I responded, "Daddy, I did what I did for God. If I had been doing it for you, I would have quit because it was too hard."

There were so many lessons in my thirties, but problem-solving, commitment, and the value of persistence are the top three.

Forties – 2002 - 2011

The last few years of my thirties were transitional. Lenny and I were restoring our marriage, which had suffered greatly while I was running the ministry. We moved to Virginia, and I landed back in hospitality. I will always believe the learning moments of the previous decade provided me with a solid foundation as a leader and corporate executive. However, it is my faith to believe that my unwavering commitment to the ministry and God's calling on my life resulted in blessings that came in the way of opportunity, promotions, and financial gain. In 2005, I went to work for Crescent Hotels and Resorts in my first above-property role. Lenny and I bought our first home together, and we were enjoying our first granddaughter.

If you can't count on anything else in life, you can count on life doing what life does. Just like the tide ebbs and flows, such is life. One of my spiritual fathers, Roscoe Conner, once said, "Everyone wants to be on the mountaintop, but without the toiling in the valley, the view would not be as beautiful from the mountaintop."

In 2010, I felt a tug in my spirit that I had not felt in a long time. I knew I had to get focused on my spirituality. I needed a traditional church family – something I had not had since I was in my grand-daddy's church in China Grove, North Carolina. One of my first speaking engagements was leading the Wednesday night testimony service at six years old. I decided to become a catholic convert and enrolled in RCIA to begin my journey to Catholicism.

Fifties – 2012 – 2022

If the thirties were the most challenging decade, the fifties were the most humbling. That said, a little dose of humility is perfect for the soul.

Lenny retired at 62, and we were living out our plan for him to support my career growth and take care of me and our home. Less than two years later, at 53, I quit my job with Crescent after ten years and started my own business. I should have been better prepared financially before jumping into my own company, but with my mother's voice ringing in my ear saying, "You can do anything you set your mind to," somehow, I survived the next four years as an entrepreneur.

During that same time, my son-in-law was deployed to England for three years and then South Korea for three more. My relation-ship with my daughter was in trouble, and the distance between us made it difficult to repair the issues. Lenny's mom came to live with us for a short while, and he became her caregiver for the next six years.

Suddenly, life was doing what life does on many fronts, and I was crumbling under the weight of it. One of the worst and best things that ever happened to me was what came next. I was diagnosed with depression. Coming from a ministerial background, therapy was taboo, but I needed help. Never in a million years would I have thought I would be diagnosed with depression, but the car ride home from my first therapy session was an awakening. I am very grateful for the diagnosis because it set me on a path of self-care that has become my way of life. My three-legged stool consists of prayer/meditation, exercise, and a healthy diet. My 55-year-old body was much healthier than the 30-year-old one!

But wait, my fiftieth decade was only half over, and there is still a worldwide pandemic looming in the future. As I stated before, that which doesn't kill you only makes you stronger.

In January 2019, I received a call about a position with PM Hotel Group, and even though my business had taken off and that year was shaping up to be the best year since I started the company, I took the job. A true God moment! Our survival of 2020 and 2021 would have looked a lot different without the steady income provided by my job.

In addition to the humility during my fiftieth decade, it was a new beginning. My most significant ah-ha moment was realizing you cannot allow a job to define you. Additionally, I was able to learn so much from the challenges of relationships, sacrifice, and recovery. Compassion for myself helped me recognize my vulnerabilities and find the shore after the storm. The healing was beautiful for my mind, body, and spirit.

The transitional moment was becoming the mentor and not the mentee. It is fulfilling to see my 20-, 30-, or 40-year-old self in younger men and women and provide advice born from life and professional experience. The role reversal of caring for parents who always cared for us and being able to step up for them is an honor. I am grateful for all of that but most thankful for the awesome relationship I have found with God. All the diet and exercise in the world will not keep my body from breaking down, but my soul will live forever. These days, I find myself spending more and more time with spiritual nourishment.

Everyone has a past that has shaped the story of their life. Your journey will have many twists and turns and may not always be easy. There will be joy, and there will be sorrow. Sometimes, you feel like you could sprout wings and fly and, at other times, find it hard to place one foot before the other. You cannot change history; even if you could, you would have to give up the greatness to erase the mistakes. I encourage you to reflect on the decades that built you. Celebrate the accomplishments and own the mistakes. Turn every mistake or poor decision you make in your journey into a learning moment. There will be times in your life when you will learn what to do, and other times you will know what not to do. Keep learning and using those lessons to become a stronger, more authentic you. And if you take nothing else away from this chapter, always remember to show gratitude and forgiveness to the people who have been part of your story. There will be people who encourage you – be grateful for those. Others will try to hinder your progress – forgive them. Forgiveness is very liberating. Lastly, always show yourself the same grace you have for others. Remember, you are only human.

Recently, someone asked me a fundamental question. If you live to be 90, then you have only lived one-half of your adult life. What do you plan to do with the second half? I am unsure what that is yet, but I know a few things: you are never too old to learn or reinvent yourself. So, never stop dreaming and keep your bucket list long.

TAKEAWAYS

1. **Embrace Change and Challenges**: This chapter underscores the importance of embracing life's changes and challenges. It's clear that every tough situation, like taking charge of a family crisis or starting a new venture, holds valuable lessons and opportunities for growth. Adversity is not a roadblock but a stepping stone to greater resilience. Facing challenges head-on builds character and often leads to unexpected rewards and personal development.

2. **Value of Family and Relationships**: Relationships, whether they are with family, friends, or colleagues, are complex and require effort. Entering into relationships means dealing with the good and the baggage that comes with it. The importance of creating and maintaining a stable family life, as experienced with a supportive partner and extended family, provides a nurturing environment that's foundational for both personal happiness and overcoming life's obstacles.

3. **Persistence Pays Off**: The relentless pursuit of goals, despite setbacks, is a powerful lesson. My journey through the hospitality industry without a college education highlights how determination and hard work can be rewarded. Persistence is not just about stubbornly pushing forward; it's about continuously learning, adapting, and striving for excellence in one's chosen field.

4. **Self-Care and Mental Health**: The revelation and subsequent treatment of depression demonstrates the critical importance of self-care and mental health awareness. It reminds us that seeking help is not a weakness but a courageous step towards healing. Balancing life with a

regimen of prayer, meditation, exercise, and a healthy diet is essential for both physical and mental well-being.

5. **Lifelong Learning**: Whether formal education or life experiences, learning is a continuous process. Every phase of life offers unique lessons that contribute to personal and professional growth. It is never too late to learn new skills, switch careers, or even change personal beliefs, as evidenced by my spiritual journey and career advancements.

6. **Authenticity and Integrity**: Being true to yourself is crucial for personal satisfaction and integrity. My advice to lead authentically, stay true to one's values, and not allow work or others to define you is a powerful call to live with sincerity. Authenticity fosters genuine relationships and a life that resonates with one's deepest values and beliefs.

7. **The Role of Gratitude and Forgiveness**: Gratitude and forgiveness are potent tools for personal liberation and peace. I encourage you to be thankful for those who support you and to forgive those who may have hindered you. Holding on to resentment binds us to the past, while forgiveness frees us to experience the present and embrace the future.

8. **The Unpredictability of Life**: The certainty of life's ebbs and flows, as symbolized by the changing tides, calls for adaptability and faith. Be prepared for the unexpected and find strength in the face of uncertainty. Life will have its ups and downs, but maintaining hope and a positive outlook can guide us through the most challenging times.

The chapter underscores the importance of these lessons through a life rich in experiences, both positive and negative. Each decade brought its own challenges and teachings, emphasizing the significance of self-awareness, adaptability, and a relentless spirit in navigating the journey of life.

REFLECTIONS

"You are the one that possesses the keys to your being. You carry the passport to your own happiness."

Diane von Furstenberg

CHAPTER THREE

Charting Uncharted Waters

Captain Amber de Nooijer, Viking River Cruises

When I first met Amber, my husband and I were enjoying Viking River Cruises' Rhine River getaway for my 60th birthday. It was our first night, and we were in the lounge for our safety briefing. The program director, Alan Custovic, greeted us and told us what to expect for the next eight days. As the agenda continued, he introduced the hotel manager, Mohamed Safwat. He continued the orientation by providing an overview of the stateroom and services we would enjoy during our journey. From where I was sitting, I could not see the participants until they were introduced and entered the room. Now, it was time for the program director to introduce the captain. At the same time, I heard him say, "Please welcome your captain for the journey, Captain Amber Nooijer." I saw this young woman in uniform come walking in. I could not help myself; I said out loud, "Lead like a girl!"

I was impressed at first sight but even more impressed after I heard the story of Captain Amber, a 27-year-old woman who would sail our ship for the next week.

Amber grew up in the Netherlands. She lived with her mom and sister. At 15 years old, she graduated high school, and it was time to determine what technical skill she would learn. Amber did not start out wanting to be a sailor; she wanted to be a baker. So,

Amber's mom took her to see the bakery school and register. When Amber saw the other students covered in flour from head to toe and learned she would have to report to school every morning at 5:00 AM, she quickly abandoned the idea of being a baker.

At this point, Amber was without a plan. Fortunately, Amber's mom was not settling for the no-plan circumstances and required Amber to pick another trade to learn. I can just see this likely heated battle between mom and a 15-year-old girl. Amber said she literally had her tablet in her hand one day during one of these mother/daughter discussions and said, "Okay, fine, I will choose something." She scrolled through the list on her tablet and randomly stuck her finger on one of the trade schools listed. Her finger landed on sailing school. Wow! That is one way to decide a career path, I guess.

At 15 years old, Amber started sailing school. The two-year course consisted of eight weeks in a classroom, and the rest of the lessons were on board a ship. Her first ship was a 445-foot tanker, where she was the only female, and the rest of her shipmates were 25- to 30-year-old men. She lived, learned, and worked alongside these men day in and day out.

At this point in the interview, I asked Amber how she survived the circumstances. I could only envision a very scared and intimidated teenage girl. Thankfully, Amber's mom had instilled in her a strong belief system, which included telling Amber as she was growing up, "Never let them see you sweat." The lessons learned in childhood would prove to come in handy during the time Amber spent onboard a ship.

Thirty days into her time onboard, a drunk sailor – as a joke – was going to throw her overboard. Amber did not show fear but instead punched him in the face as hard as she could. The injuries of the drunk sailor required a police report and resulted in Amber being removed from the ship. In the aftermath of this unfortunate event, Amber called more than 45 ships, trying to get someone to allow her to continue her education in sailing. Each time she heard "no," or that she was too young, or that she was a girl, or that as a teenager, she would constantly be on her phone. Fortunately, Amber was persistent; her mother advocated for her daughter and also made calls. Finally, her mom found a captain who agreed to let her continue her classes on his ship.

Amber's technical training and the beginning of her career was on a tanker. At 18 years old, she moved over to a passenger ship. Life was good for Amber; she grew to love the river and her career in sailing. But things were also happening in Amber's personal life; she was dating and soon committed to a relationship with her life partner. When Amber became pregnant with her daughter, she assumed her career choices would need to change. After 16 weeks of maternity leave, she had no choice but to return to work, so she accepted a job on a ferry. She sailed from point A to point B and returned, completing an eight-hour shift day after day and returning home to her new family. She stayed in this job for three years. She describes this time in her life as a disaster. Sailing from the same point A to point B was boring for Amber. By her own admission, when she is bored, it is not only not suitable for her but also unsuitable for those around her. She expressed to her partner how unhappy she was with her job and found he was willing to support her in returning to the river and passenger ships.

Two weeks after this discussion, Viking called Amber and asked her to return, but they wanted her to return as captain this time. Amber agreed to return, but recognizing that being the captain of a passenger ship comes with a great deal of responsibility for the crew and passengers aboard, she requested to come back as the first officer. Viking agreed, but only until the end of the year. Five months later, Amber became the captain of the Viking Mani and sailed the Rhine.

I asked Amber how she manages the two weeks on and two weeks off schedule, balancing her personal life and her career. She said, "I must be good at compartmentalizing. I do not call home every day during the two weeks I am on the ship; otherwise, I would miss my family too much. The time at home is all about my family." Amber had to set herself up for success, so she moved to Romania, where her partner's family is. As such, when she commutes to the ship in Amsterdam, it is a day's journey, and she is responsible for most of the travel expenses. She didn't complain; she said she uses the time to decompress from the ship and be ready to be a mom and partner.

As the captain, she leads a nautical team of ten men. She shared that only once in her eight-month career did someone get out of line and disrespect her position because she was a woman. Amber handled it by addressing it head-on and setting a standard that this behavior would not be tolerated. I asked what she loved most about her career as a captain, and she said the people and the stress. Stress? She went on to say she loves solving problems. Whether it is sailing a river drying up, getting emergency medical attention for a passenger, or delivering 180 passengers safely home, she never lets them see her sweat.

Interesting side note: I asked Amber if her father was in her life, and she shared that he was not so much when she was growing up, but as an adult, she has rekindled a relationship with her dad. He, too, sails, and her career has provided a commonality for them to build on.

TAKEAWAYS

1. **Embrace Flexibility in Career Choices**: Amber's initial desire to be a baker shifted dramatically when she discovered the realities of that profession. This teaches us the importance of being open to change and the willingness to pivot when our expectations don't match reality. Embracing flexibility allows us to explore opportunities we might have never considered, leading to potentially fulfilling career paths.

2. **The Importance of Family Support and Advocacy**: Amber's mother played a critical role in her choice of career and persistence in the face of adversity. Family can provide both the push to explore new possibilities and the support needed to persevere through challenges. This lesson underlines the value of having a supportive network, whether it's family or a chosen family of friends and mentors.

3. **Resilience in the Face of Discrimination and Danger**: Facing discrimination and a life-threatening situation early in her career, Amber's resolve to stand up for herself and not show fear is a powerful lesson in resilience. It's important to advocate for yourself and maintain your dignity and safety, especially in environments where discrimination or harassment may occur.

4. **The Power of Persistence**: After being removed from her first ship, Amber's determination to continue her education by calling over 45 ships teaches the virtue of persistence. Rejection is often not an end but a hurdle to overcome. The willingness to persistently pursue one's goals is often what separates those who achieve their ambitions from those who do not.

5. **Work-Life Balance Requires Strategic Choices**: Amber's move to Romania to be closer to family support while managing her schedule of two weeks on and two weeks off shows strategic life planning. This emphasizes the need for balance and the sometimes tough decisions required to maintain it, especially in demanding careers.

6. **Leadership Through Composure and Directness**: Amber's management style of not showing stress and addressing disrespect head-on showcases effective leadership. Good leaders must maintain their composure in high-pressure situations and confront issues directly to set a clear standard for their team's behavior and performance.

7. **Finding Fulfillment in Challenge and Problem-Solving**: Amber's love for the stress of her job and the problems she gets to solve indicates that fulfillment can come from overcoming challenges. This suggests that seeking out roles that challenge us, rather than those that offer comfort and routine, can lead to greater job satisfaction and personal growth.

8. **Shared Interests Can Bridge Estranged Relationships**: Amber's reconnection with her father through their shared interest in sailing shows that finding common ground can help mend strained relationships. It underscores the idea that it's never too late to rebuild connections, and shared passions can be a strong foundation for renewed bonds.

Captain Amber de Nooijer's journey beautifully intertwines these lessons, portraying a multifaceted tale of determination, resilience, support, balance, responsibility, passion, and connection, providing a rich tapestry of insights. Her story is not just about charting uncharted waters in her career but also about navigating the complexities of life with courage and integrity. Her journey is inspirational, showing that with enough grit and support, it's possible to overcome stereotypes and achieve success on one's own terms.

REFLECTIONS

*"Optimism is the faith that leads to achievement.
Nothing can be done without hope and confidence."*
Helen Keller

CHAPTER FOUR

Trailblazers for Equality

From Abigail Adams to Nikki Haley

I am so grateful that when God created me, he decided I should be female. I love the feminine attributes that come with being a woman. Empathy, intuition, emotional intelligence, and collaboration in leadership can be very powerful. I am personally grateful for the gift of Southern charm. It is true; you can catch more flies with honey than with vinegar. That said, some people would see these attributes as weaknesses and perceive women as less powerful than the men in the organization.

Today, it is not even just a battle of the sexes. There are varying points of view and backgrounds in the office environment, and the most essential attribute can be empathy and the ability to meet people where they are instead of where you think they should be.

I recognize that women are often more vulnerable and less likely to stand up for themselves. We are often the peacemakers, which can be perceived as avoiding conflict when it is just a different and better form of negotiation.

Recently, in a conversation with a young woman I coach, I asked her about a situation that did not align with her morals. She responded, "I just figure that's how it will always be." I found that interesting, knowing her convictions related to her faith and the circumstances that were challenging her religious beliefs. Like many women, my client was conditioned to feel there are times when we must accept, and there is no opportunity to be a change-maker. What I heard in that young woman's comment was defeat. Her statement said, "I do not believe I can make a difference; therefore, I must accept that this is just how it is going to be."

What if the great women who blazed a path for us had just decided, "I can't make a difference, so why try, or it will cost me more than I am willing to give if I take a stand?" We can learn from our history, be confident we can make a difference in our current circumstances, and create a brighter future enriched by inclusion for women and people from all cultures.

Abigail and John Adams were known as America's first power couple. In a letter dated March 31, 1776, Mrs. Adams wrote a letter to her husband asking him not to forget about the nation's women when fighting for America's independence from England.[2]

One hundred fifty years after Abigail Adams wrote the letter to her husband, on August 26, 1920, the 19th Amendment was voted in, and women could finally vote. However, it still had restrictions. It was not until 1965 that President Lyndon B. Johnson signed the 19th Amendment Act that would ban restrictions for literacy testing, poll tax, and other clauses grandfathered in.[3] The action of President Johnson had an immediate impact. By the end of 1965, a quarter of a million new black voters had been registered to vote. By the end of 1966, only four out of 13 southern states had fewer than 50 percent of African Americans registered to vote. The Voting Rights Act of 1965 was readopted and strengthened in 1970, 1975, and 1982.[4]

Wage Equity

By the early 20th century, one-fourth of the American workforce was women. During World War II in 1942, with the men deployed, women replaced men in the factories and other jobs. The National War Labor Board voted in favor of equal pay for women when they were replacing male workers. In 1960, women still earned less than two-thirds of their male counterparts.[5]

Not all women were willing to sit back and accept a salary of two-thirds of their male counterparts as a win (pun intended). Thirty-nine-time grand slam winner Billie Jean King did not back off in the face of social injustice when women made far less than men.

The Open Era of tennis as we know it today started in 1968, allowing amateurs and professionals to compete for prize money. The wage gap was blatant! In 1970, Ilie Nastase was paid $3,500, and Billie Jean King earned only $600. In her first Wimbledon, she made 37% of what the male champion won.

Ms. King was also the founder of the Women's Tennis Association (WTA) and Women's Sports Federation. The WTA was formed when she barricaded with 63 other players in the Gloucester Hotel in London and threatened to boycott the US Open later that year. Ban deodorant gave a grant to the tournament, and that year, both the male and female champions were paid $25,000.

It still took years for other tournaments to follow suit. The Australian Open joined the equal pay movement in 1984 but separated from the movement in 1996 through 2000. The French Open started in 2006, and finally Wimbledon in 2007. Apparently, the men and women have both gained ground, given the payout for the US Open was $3,000,000 in 2023.[6]

Billie Jean King made another massive statement for equality for women when she agreed to participate in The Battle of the Sexes.

Her opponent, Bobby Riggs, was famously chauvinistic and stated publicly, "Women belong in the bedroom and kitchen, in that order. He said, "I'll tell you why I'll win; she is a woman, and they do not have the emotional stability. She'll choke."[7]

But she didn't "choke," she smoked him and won in a straight set, 6-4, 6-3, 6-3, taking home a $100,000 paycheck. The only thing Riggs had to say then was, "I should have taken her more seriously." [8]

As 2024 looms on the horizon, women have certainly experienced significant setbacks because of COVID-19.[9]

- 47 million additional women and girls were pushed into poverty worldwide.

- In a poll of 16 countries, women are responsible for 29% more childcare per week than men.

- One in two women reported they know someone or have themselves experienced violence since the start of the pandemic (13 countries polled).

- In the hospitality industry, 57% of those who left were women. In many cases, they made less money than their male partner and, therefore, were selected to stay home and care for the children or elderly parents.

The culture of women not being treated as equals has deep roots and goes as far back as the Bible. Case in point, the Book of John, in the 8th chapter, tells the story of a woman who was brought to Jesus by the teachers of the law and the Pharisees. She was accused of committing adultery, and they stood her before Jesus. They were testing Jesus by reminding him of the Law of Moses; they were trying to trap him. However, there is a back story here. If the Law of Moses required a woman caught in the act of adultery, what did it require of the man who also participated in the same act? The story has a wonderful ending and depicts Jesus as a great role model for leaders. Throughout his ministry, he consistently exhibited confidence, empathy, and compassion. Rather than allowing the Pharisees to trap him, he simply said, "Let any of you who is without sin be the first to throw a stone at her." When they heard this, they began to leave one by one. Jesus did not condemn her but forgave her and directed her to "go and sin no more."

As women, we have won many battles, but perhaps the war for equality has not yet been won. However, we are gaining ground.

Recently, I was changing planes at the Charlotte Douglas International Airport, and a public announcement from the mayor, Vi Lyles, was welcoming visitors to the "Queen City." I smiled and whispered to myself, "Lead like a girl."

As a country music fan, I am delighted to see the remarkable women of country come together, lifting each other up and calling for equal airtime and recognition of their talent. One of my favorite headliners today is Lainey Wilson. She is a shining example of resilience for young women everywhere to never stop chasing their dreams. Wilson tried out for *American Idol* seven times before being selected to participate; even then, she did not make it past the first round.[10] At least she did not let that discourage her from chasing her dream. Her resilience and persistence paid off. She turned her setback into a comeback; today, she is one of the top entertainers in country music and holds the title of 2023 Entertainer of the Year.[11]

Nikki Haley showed that women can indeed be as strong as men. Her autobiography, *With All Due Respect: Defending America with Grit and Grace*, a New York Times bestseller, introduces a woman of immigrant parents from a male-dominated culture who rises in the ranks of state and local politics, taking her all the way to the United Nations under the Trump administration.[12] I applaud her for capitalizing on the platform her position presented and using her voice to call out not just equality for women but equality for all humanity. I hope we have not heard the last of Ms. Haley.

For years, the percentage of female CEOs in a Fortune 500 company was stuck at 8%. In January 2023, the Society of Human Resource Managers website shared an article by Fortune reporting the percentage now exceeds 10%. That seems like a small win, but a quote from the article by Jane Stevenson, who is vice chair, board & CEO services, global leader, CEO succession practice at Korn Ferry, points out it is becoming more normal than an oddity and, therefore, "less risky, subconsciously, to put a woman in the top spot."[13]

Through my research for this book and my own professional experiences, I am grateful for the men I have known and learned about who are not threatened by women or driven by ego in their decisions to promote and support the growth of women in executive positions. To all the mothers and fathers, like mine, of daughters, encouraging them to chase their dreams until they become a reality, hats off to you!

As the author of this book, I do not want to pit the girls against the boys further but to encourage collaboration and a corporate culture that allows us to learn from one another. We should see every colleague as a teammate, regardless of gender or race, as someone who can help us succeed when working together. We ARE better together! After all, almost everything in life is better with a village than trying to go it alone.

TAKEAWAYS

1. **Embrace Feminine Qualities as Strengths**: Traditional feminine attributes like empathy, emotional intelligence, and collaboration are not weaknesses but are powerful tools in leadership. Women like Abigail Adams utilized these traits effectively in their advocacy, influencing critical moments in history. Recognizing and valuing these characteristics can reshape perceptions of power and leadership, showing that success is not about abandoning your inherent qualities but leveraging them to foster change and inspire others.

2. **Never Underestimate the Power of Persistence**: The path to equality is laden with obstacles, but relentless persistence can lead to breakthroughs. The story of Billie Jean King, who fought for and eventually secured equal prize money for women in tennis, demonstrates that challenging the status quo requires a steadfast commitment to one's goals. Her victory in the "Battle of the Sexes" is a testament to how tenacity can not only triumph over prejudice but can also significantly alter public opinion and pave the way for future advancements.

3. **Legal Rights are Critical to Progress**: The evolution of the 19th Amendment shows that legal rights are a cornerstone of achieving equality. It wasn't until the Voting Rights Act of 1965 that the full intention of the amendment was realized, demonstrating that laws need to be comprehensive and actively enforced to dismantle systemic barriers. This legal groundwork is essential for the equitable participation of women in all societal aspects, from voting to workplace equality.

4. **Role Models and Mentors Matter**: Individuals like

Nikki Haley serve as crucial role models for young women, showing that with grit and determination, it's possible to overcome cultural and gender biases to achieve high leadership positions. Having a diverse range of role models from different backgrounds and industries helps to inspire the next generation. It also provides tangible examples of what can be achieved, thereby expanding the realm of what women consider possible for their own lives.

5. **Equality is Still a Work in Progress**: Despite significant advancements, the battle for full equality has not yet been won, as evidenced by setbacks during the COVID-19 pandemic. The statistics of increased poverty among women and the disproportionate burden of care women faced highlight that progress can be fragile and must be vigilantly protected and advanced.

6. **The Value of Inclusion**: Learning from different perspectives and backgrounds enriches the workplace and society at large. The increasing number of women in executive positions is a positive trend that not only benefits corporate culture but also sets a precedent that paves the way for more inclusivity. As barriers are broken down, it becomes less risky and more normalized for women to occupy top roles.

7. **Championing Equality is Everyone's Responsibility**: The journey toward equality is not just a women's issue; it is a societal goal that requires the active participation of all genders. Men who support and promote the growth of women in leadership positions demonstrate that gender equality benefits everyone and that the most successful teams are those that value diversity and inclusive collaboration.

8. **Resilience in the Face of Adversity**: Lainey Wilson's story of overcoming rejection and pursuing her dreams with resilience highlights the importance of perseverance. Setbacks can be reframed as steps to success when met with persistence and determination. This lesson serves as a powerful reminder that even in the face of adversity, staying true to one's goals and continuing to push forward can lead to remarkable achievements.

These lessons highlight the progress made in the fight for gender equality and the challenges that remain. They emphasize the importance of understanding, collaboration, and resilience in continuing this fight.

REFLECTIONS

"The future belongs to those who believe in the beauty of their dreams."

Eleanor Roosevelt

CHAPTER FIVE

Breaking Free from Self-Imposed Limitations

O ne of the most significant issues for women in a corporate environment is confidence. To cure this flaw in our psyche, we must first understand why. Once we understand why we hold ourselves back for lack of confidence, we can learn to recognize the land mines and come up with solutions to address them.

Let's return to that little girl in the formative years of zero to eight. It is very likely you are a victim of your parents' and grand-parents' glass ceilings. I have already introduced you to my two grandmothers who had very different views of how women should behave. I grew up the epitome of a true southern belle – beauty pageants and a cheerleader; if my mother could have afforded it, I am pretty sure I could add debutant to that list. Every year before the pageant at school, we would make an appointment at the Clinique counter for me to hone my skills of applying makeup. Don't misunderstand; I wasn't forced to do these things; I loved every minute of it! Until I was in my thirties, I would not even go to the 7-Eleven without a full face of makeup on. Silly, don't you think? Somewhere in all the catwalks and cheerleading tryouts, I began to believe my success was very much about my outward appearance.

While we can certainly use our sexy to our advantage, it is a tool but not a confidence builder. In fact, leaning on our outward appearance too much can create ebbs and flows in our confidence level as our bodies and external appearance change.

Too much focus on our outward appearance can also create another obstacle: women being jealous of other women. Have you ever wondered why the "Good Ole Boys" club is so successful? They don't care who has the best hair day or whose outfit is the chicest, and they certainly do not notice if one of the guys puts on a few pounds. When I was in my twenties, I was a size two. I cannot tell you how many times other women would say to me, "Oh my God, you are so skinny." Really? People come in all shapes and sizes, and before we put on eyeliner, the latest fashion trend, or step into those red pumps, we must be comfortable in our own skin.

As women, we are very emotional creatures, but we need to know when to bring it and when to leave it at home. Passion, com-passion, and empathy are welcome in any decision or situation. But let's talk about tears in the workplace. I cry when I am happy, mad, or sad. Many things can move me to tears. Tears can make people uncomfortable, especially the men in the room. Crying too often can be perceived as a weakness. One of my favorite quotes from *Steel Magnolias* is, "Laughter through tears is my favorite emotion." Laughing until you cry is always acceptable! The sad and mad tears can be more controversial. Let's break it down. There is a difference between being "moved" to tears or "reduced" to tears. Being moved to tears when someone is winning an award, or you hear a story of someone fighting through a disability to overcome is perfectly fine. Tissue, please! But being reduced to tears is crying because someone hurt your feelings or made you mad, and it is usually best not to let others push your buttons like that. We will have a whole chapter on your buttons. But for now, I recommend breathing techniques and focusing on how you will address the jerk in the room later in private and take yourself out of the moment and into a place of control. That said, sometimes you cannot control the waterworks, and in those cases, no apology is needed. Leave the situation and find a private place to pull it back together. Weakness only happens if you let that moment pass without going back and addressing the person in the room who reduced you to tears. This leads me to another reason women lack confidence: we are terrible at advocating for ourselves.

In 1963, the Equal Pay Act was signed by President John F. Kennedy.[14] Yet today, 60 years later, we are still not equally compensated, and statistics show it will take until 2085 for women to earn equal pay compared to men. I believe one of the biggest reasons for that, in many cases, is the boys ask and we don't. Why is that? Are we accepting it? Maybe we think our boss should recognize our greatness and be moved to shower us with rewards. Yeah, right! It doesn't work like that. You have not because you ask not. Often, we get caught up in our own heads, and that keeps us from going after what we deserve. The voices in our heads say that we still need to prove ourselves, we are not qualified, or we lack education or experience. That inner voice chips away at confidence and needs to be silenced once and for all. Let's see how those thoughts can become confidence builders instead of barriers. *"I have a proven track record. I am qualified to do my job. I am highly skilled and bring a wealth of knowledge to my role."* When you retrain your inner voice, not only will you build your confidence, but you will also start to believe you deserve, you can, and you will. Besides, if you don't take care of yourself, who will?

I was fortunate to have a mother who always told me I could do whatever I set my mind to. I would say most women buy into that belief. However, the thoughts right behind that are often what hold us back. The thought is that to do whatever we set our minds to comes with choices, and the choices are very often important life choices. Can I have children and a career? What if my career requires travel or relocation? How will my career choices affect my responsibility to my family? Abraham Lincoln once said, "In the end, it's not the years in your life that count. It's the life in your years." Remember, you are navigating your life's journey, and any choices should only be because you set the goal that determines the most desired outcome. At least once each year, a person should find 48 hours of quiet time to reflect on the previous year's accomplishments and look ahead to align priorities and goals based on the storied history. Trust me, your dreams and goals will age along with you. What was important at twenty or thirty will not be the same in your forties and fifties. So don't try to plan too far ahead; it will be for naught. One of my favorite sayings is, "If you want to make God laugh, tell him your plans."

Imposter Syndrome

The National Institute of Health defines imposter syndrome as a behavioral health phenomenon described as self-doubt of intellect, skills, or accomplishments among high-achieving individuals. Perfectionism, superheroism, fear of failure, denial of competence and capability, and fear of failure are all or part of the belief system of someone who embodies imposter syndrome.[15]

Do you suffer from any of these self-imposed labels? If so, it is important that you recognize and address them. Hiring a business coach can help you identify these opportunities for improvement. It will be imperative to address them if you aspire to grow your career. A belief system of self-doubt will hijack your career goals by diminishing your confidence.

In 2005, when I started my first multi-property role, I found myself in board rooms where much of the conversation was over my head. In almost every meeting, I would have an imposter syndrome moment. I would find myself thinking, how did I get here? My only degree was a GSD, "Get Stuff Done." At the time, I had no idea how many CEOs had no degree and moved up in their careers based on their work ethic, abilities, and vision.

I recommend higher education, but if that is not in the cards for you, do not hold yourself back or temper your goals. You do not always need a degree to achieve the career you aspire to have. If your career goals do require a certification or college degree, then I encourage you to follow the path of some of the women, like Joy and Martha, interviewed in this book and go for it. You are never too old to learn.

Another reason I experienced imposter syndrome was from the types of conversations in meetings. In many cases, I was trying to convince investors and owners I had the skill set to meet the investment goals for their hotel. I was almost one hundred percent leaning into my sales skills versus my knowledge of the data and how achievable it was. It was a slippery slope. Most of the conversations were centered around deal terms, cap rates, and exit strategies, an area of the business I did not fully understand at the time.

Remember this: you are never smarter than when you realize what you *don't* know. In those moments when you feel like everything is over your head, ask questions or take notes and do the research later. Do not let frustration and insecurity take over and cost you a learning opportunity. Even today, with all of my experience, I often lean over to the person sitting next to me in a meeting and ask what something means. There is no shame in recognizing what you do not know. You have likely heard the analogy – the only stupid question is the one never asked.

If you are there, it is because you belong and have earned your seat at the table. In these instances, recognize you are not only a contributor but also a student. I love this quote by Tao Te Ching, "When the student is ready, the teacher will appear. When the student is truly ready... The teacher will disappear."[16] It is important to take full advantage of the teachers in your life and career, the ones that appear "when you are ready." Do not be ashamed to say, I do not know, then listen and learn.

Today, I sometimes ask myself the same question. How did I get here? However, when I ask myself that question today, it is not centered around imposter syndrome; it is of immense gratitude. I am counting my blessings: I am accomplished, and God has shown me favor. There may be people at the table who have more power than me, but I have the benefit of favor, and that is a beautiful thing. I will always choose favor over power.

Luke 1:28 – The angel went to her and said, "Greetings, you who are highly favored! The Lord is with you."

Every fiber of my being exudes confidence. I was raised with "pull your bootstraps up and walk in that room like you own it" parenting. If I had to sum up myself, it starts with what my parents taught me in those two little phrases used over and over in my life. That said, I exude confidence until I don't, and in the moments when I doubt my abilities or my confidence wanes, I find it fostered by the voices in my head or allowing others to determine how I feel. Those are the land mines I referenced earlier in this chapter. Once realized, you will find you recognize them and address them before they do too much damage to the Wonder Woman roaring inside of you.

TAKEAWAYS

1. **Recognize the Influence of Childhood Conditioning**: Childhood experiences and cultural conditioning can shape our self-perception and confidence levels. It is essential to acknowledge that the standards and expectations imposed on us during our formative years can lead to a fixation on appearance and external validation. To break free from these imprinted limitations, we need to critically examine these early influences and actively work towards defining our own measures of self-worth and success beyond superficial attributes.

2. **Utilize Personal Attributes Wisely, But Don't Rely on Them**: While leveraging our outward appeal can be advantageous in some situations, relying on it for confidence is precarious and unsustainable. As our appearances change over time, self-esteem based on looks can fluctuate, leading to instability in how we perceive ourselves. Confidence should be rooted in intrinsic qualities and achievements rather than being anchored to something as transient as physical appearance.

3. **Manage Emotions Intelligently in the Workplace**: It is paramount to understand the role of emotions in a professional setting. While passion, compassion, and empathy can enhance decision-making and workplace relationships, the display of emotions such as tears can be misconstrued and affect our professional image. Developing strategies to handle emotions effectively, such as breathing techniques or addressing issues privately, can help maintain professionalism and demonstrate emotional intelligence.

4. **Advocate for Yourself and Your Worth**: Women often

struggle with self-advocacy, which can hinder our professional advancement and contribute to ongoing disparities in pay and recognition. It's critical to silence the internal voice that undermines our capabilities and replace it with affirmations of our qualifications and contributions. By doing so, we can better negotiate for what we deserve and close the confidence gap that hampers self-advocacy.

5. **Plan for the Present, Not Just the Future**: I encourage living in the moment and making choices that reflect current goals and values rather than being overly concerned with distant future plans. This approach can prevent becoming paralyzed by the pressure of long-term planning and allows for a more responsive and fulfilling path that adapts to life's changes. Regular reflection on achievements and realigning priorities can ensure that our actions remain congruent with our evolving aspirations.

6. **Acknowledge and Overcome Imposter Syndrome**: Imposter syndrome can severely limit our professional growth by instilling self-doubt. Recognizing and confronting these feelings is crucial to career development. Seeking support through mentors or business coaches can help in identifying and dismantling these limiting beliefs. Realizing that even high achievers experience these doubts can normalize the phenomenon and empower individuals to push beyond it.

7. **Embrace Continuous Learning and Curiosity**: It is important to embrace our gaps in knowledge as opportunities for growth. Asking questions and seeking clarification are signs of intelligence and a commitment to learning, not incompetence. This mindset not only enhances personal development but also fosters an environment where continuous learning is valued and encouraged.

8. **Gratitude and Recognition of Favor Over Power**: As I reflect on my journey with gratitude, I recognize that favor and personal accomplishments can be more gratifying and influential than positional power. There is value in acknowledging our own hard work and blessings, and choosing to focus on the positive aspects of our career trajectory rather than solely on the hierarchical structures of power within an organization.

These lessons highlight the importance of understanding our past, building genuine self-confidence, supporting other women, expressing emotions appropriately, advocating for ourselves, making balanced life choices, and continuously reassessing our goals.

<u>REFLECTIONS</u>

"The most alluring thing a woman can have is confidence."

Beyoncé

CHAPTER SIX

Breaking Barriers and Leading with Grace

Dr. Deena Casiero, Director of Sports Medicine and Head Team Physician, University of Connecticut

I first met Deena when she was 11 years old. In 1988, I married her uncle, Lenny Casiero. I not only gained a husband, but I also gained a big Italian family. Deena, along with her eight-year-old sister Corrine, became my niece. Fortunately, we lived very close to Deena and Corrine. My daughter was the same age as Corrine, so we spent much time together as the girls were growing up.

Watching Deena grow up, she always seemed slightly older than her years. She was a great kid! Her parents, Anthony and Lola Casiero, separated when she was five. Deena and her sister lived on Maple Crest in Highland, New York, with their mother. Maple Crest was a property that had been in her father's family for many years. Previously a Catskill-style summer resort, it had become a residential community when Deena was born. Also living on Maple Crest were her paternal grandma, two great-aunts, and one great-uncle. Deena had much influence from strong Italian women. She learned the art of cooking and crafts that so many Italian women of her generation were renowned for. Deena was also good at those things; even at a young age, I watched her strive for perfection.

When Deena was growing up, there were no professionals in

her immediate family. Her mother was a first-generation Italian American, and her paternal grandmother was a third-generation Italian American. Even though Deena and her sister were raised predominantly by their mother in a single-parent home, they had a lot of family support.

As Deena entered high school, her brilliance and determination to break the glass ceiling and become the first professional in her immediate family, especially among the women, shone through. Her mother always encouraged her to go to college. When Deena was a sophomore in high school, her mother remarried, and just one month after the marriage, Deena's stepfather died in his sleep, and the family became three again. In 1993, her mother met Howard Finkelstein, an attorney, who would eventually become her stepfather. Her mother and stepfather, Howard, were her biggest supporters and had the most powerful influence on her success.

Deena and I had very similar childhoods; our parents divorced when we were very young, and our primary residence was in our mother's home. Both of our mothers were strong, determined, and good providers, but they had to work hard, and sometimes the struggle was great. It came as no surprise to me when I asked Deena why she had so much drive to succeed, and she stated, "Growing up, I knew I never wanted to have to rely on a man to support me, and I never wanted to struggle financially."

In the fall of 1995, Deena entered Springfield College. Four years later, Deena graduated magna cum laude with a Bachelor of Science in athletic training and a minor in sports psychology. I remember her graduation day and the celebration. It was an excellent accomplishment for Deena and a milestone for the family.

When Deena was in high school, she tore her ACL playing basketball. Unfortunately, as a sophomore in college, she tore the ACL in her other knee and had to have several more surgeries over the next two years. While recovering from these injuries, Deena became increasingly interested in the human body, how it works, and how it heals. In her senior year of college, Deena questioned whether a career as an athletic trainer would truly fulfill her desire in sports medicine. Deena said, "It started to become evident to me that this path would only leave me wanting more." While it seemed she was headed in the right direction, Deena had a new and bigger vision. Deena wanted to be a doctor.

During the graduation party honoring her achievements at Springfield College, I remember hearing that Deena was returning to school to get her MD. It came as no surprise to me!

Deena wasted no time in starting the studies needed to accomplish her goal. She pursued a post-baccalaureate program for two years at Stony Brook University in Long Island. Following her studies there, she sat for the Medical College Admission Test (MCAT) and began the year-long process of applying to medical schools.

She also worked as an athletic trainer at Mattituck High School that year. The girls' soccer coach at the high school was also the women's basketball coach at St. Joseph's College in Patchogue, New York. He recognized the quality of Deena's work, and just a few months into her job with the high school, he asked her to come to work with him at the college.

Deena was accepted to New York Medical College in Valhalla and, in 2006, received her Doctor of Medicine degree. After medical school, she completed a three-year residency in internal medicine at Montefiore Medical Center in the Bronx. Finally, she completed her primary care sports medicine fellowship at the University of Connecticut in the summer of 2010.

In September 2010, at 33, Deena started her first position as a medical doctor with ProHealth Care Associates in Lake Success, New York, as a primary care sports medicine physician in the Department of Orthopedics and Sports Medicine. She was also a team physician for Hofstra University, team physician for Molloy College, associate team physician for the NY Islanders, and tournament physician for the US Open Tennis Championship. After two years, Deena was promoted to director of sports medicine at Hofstra University and director of player medical services at the US Open Tennis Championship.

While working at ProHealth, Deena met one of her mentors, Dr. Brian Hainline, a neurologist for the practice. Neurology is not the most common pathway physicians take into the sports medicine world. Deena said, "Dr. Hainline took control of his own destiny and paved his way to a successful career in the field of sports medicine. He served as chief medical officer for the USTA from 2008-2012, and today, he is the first chief medical officer for the National Collegiate Athletic Association."

When Deena met Dr. Hainline, she soon discovered he was a huge supporter of women in executive-level positions. He watched his wife, Pascale, overcome many obstacles in her career as she tried to advance; therefore, he made a point of lifting women up, especially those who showed potential like Deena's. The US Open Tennis Championship is a tournament Dr. Hainline holds very dear to his heart. When the director, player medical services role was vacated, he strongly advocated for Deena to step into this role. In 2014, she became the first female to hold this position.

During her fellowship in 2009, she met Dr. Jeffery Anderson, director of sports medicine and head team physician at the University of Connecticut. She trained under him for 12 months, and he taught her the ins and outs of being a true team physician. Deena thought Dr. Anderson's job was her ultimate dream job. She admired how he handled his business in an incredibly demanding setting. It was evident he loved his work and showed up daily with a positive attitude, always performing his duties with grace despite the pressure. Five years later, when he stepped down, he called Deena and encouraged her to consider applying.

Deena expressed her gratitude for Dr. Anderson, saying, "Jeff recognized the potential in me. He trusted I would have the ability to navigate the political landscape in a university environment and male-dominated industry. He saw beyond my clinical knowledge and recognized my leadership abilities." In September 2015, Dr. Deena Casiero became the first female to serve as director of sports medicine and head team physician for the University of Connecticut.

In her new role, there were many landmines to navigate. Deena had to tell coaches things they did not want to hear, like their star player would need to sit out due to an injury. On many occasions, her medical judgment was called into question. Deena said, "I would wonder if they would question me the same way if I were not female." Early in her career, while traveling with a team on a charter airplane, she reports being seated in the back of the plane with the student workers while other directors and high-level administrators were sitting at the front. Indeed, she took some hits in this male-dominated industry, but she didn't let that distract her from performing her duties and continuing to grow her career. In fact, Deena proved her skills as a strong leader and decision-maker when a worldwide pandemic rocked the world of collegiate sports.

When COVID-19 showed up with a vengeance in 2020, Deena was responsible for the health and safety of approximately 650 student-athletes and staff members. NCAA rules required testing for players three times per week for some sports; however, testing was expensive and not widely available then. Additionally, the turnaround time for results was not short. Under Dr. Casiero's leadership, the sports medicine department partnered with the Human Genomics Lab on campus. The lab and sports medicine collaborated to develop a process to perform saliva-based testing in-house at the University of Connecticut. By testing in-house, they could turn the test results around in less than 24 hours, and the cost decreased from $125 to $10 per test.

In February 2021, the *Connecticut Post* highlighted Deena and UConn in an article titled "Behind the Scenes: How a Group of Scientists Made UConn Athletics Possible This Season." Dr. Casiero was quoted in the article, "It's a struggle, I think, every day," Casiero said. "But what I lean on is, my job is to take care of the athletes. My job is to make decisions I think are best."

While the testing was daunting and the workdays were long, that was not the most stressful part for Deena. During the interview, she shared what really kept her up at night. "Honestly, I did not know If I was doing the right thing. At that time, we did not know if young people would die from COVID. Looking back, we did the right thing by allowing the students to play. The most stressful part was the brutality of waiting for results and then communicating the results when positive to the players and coaches." She went on to say, "Ensuring protocol was followed and keeping them safe were always top of mind. There was no playbook for COVID."

Exhibiting incredible grace under pressure while making some very tough decisions during COVID, Deena once again showed up with a spirit of resilience, flawlessly executing her responsibilities amid the chaos. In 2022, she was promoted to the senior associate athletic director position. In this role, she leads a staff of 32, including athletic trainers, nutritionists, strength and conditioning coaches, physical therapists, and administrative staff. She is a member of the athletic director's leadership team. As such, she has been given a voice in decisions and policymaking as it pertains to the larger athletic department, going beyond just sports medicine.

Deena's career choices could not have landed her in a more male-dominated environment. At the time of this interview, only 17% of Division 1 head team physicians in the NCAA are women. That said, Deena was brilliant; she excelled in her clinical responsibilities, and people were paying attention. Good things happen for good people, and Deena benefitted from people believing in her – sometimes more than she believed in herself.

Deena fondly remembered a secret she kept to herself for many years. She spoke about one of her earliest memories during her first year of medical school. She said, "I was so afraid they were going to figure out I did not belong there. Talk about imposter syndrome!" She recognizes today that fear of failure created an underlying insecurity, which made her self-conscious – the classic symptoms of imposter syndrome.

As I concluded the interview with Deena, I asked her several questions. I encourage you to think about how you would answer these questions if they were asked of you. Learn from the lessons and ask yourself how you can apply these to your current situation.

Q: *Why did you want to become a doctor?*

A: When I made the decision to become a doctor, I simply wanted to help people. My vision of being a doctor was seeing patients and helping them recover from their injuries. I did not think about the administrative and leadership responsibilities that came with my profession. I discovered that I was also a good leader, and I was good at solving problems. I began to lean into these additional qualities I discovered about myself. When I did that, I realized there was an opportunity for me to contribute more thought leadership and participate as a policymaker within the sports medicine industry.

Q: *What are some of your favorite power moments?*

A: It is in those times when women in the sports medicine field come to me with questions because they are feeling the pressure of being in a male-dominated field, and I can provide them with insight. I have not only been in the same situation, but I have also survived it.

Q: *Do you manage the females on your team differently than the males?*

A: I am probably a little tougher on them; they face a higher level of accountability in a male-dominated field. It is not because I created it; it just exists. Therefore, I feel I have an obligation to instill confidence, empower them, and encourage them to stand up for themselves and the other women in the field. When the coach in me kicks in, I am drawn to the females with a desire to teach them how to succeed in this industry."

Q: *Was there ever a time when you experienced discrimination because you were a woman?*

A: Yes, in a previous job, I was up for a promotion to head team physician and ended up being passed over for a much younger male physician with very little experience. I had five years of experience supporting that team, so I asked why the job was offered to someone with so little experience when I felt I was more qualified. I was told that since I had just gotten married, I would want to start a family and start having children soon, so they didn't want to burden me with too much responsibility. However, he did follow that statement up with, "But the team and players love you."

Q: *Do you believe that females are gaining ground in the world of collegiate and professional sports?*

A: Current statistics say only 17% of Division 1 head team physicians are women. I think there is still much work to be done in every aspect of the sports industry. However, I am seeing a positive trend of more women as coaches, trainers, and sideline reporters for male sports. For there to be change, everyone needs to start seeing the talent and not the gender, and women need to do a better job supporting other women.

Q: *At 46, what would you tell your younger self?*

A: I would tell myself to believe in myself more. Even though I worked hard and hustled, self-confidence was an issue. All the people around me had confidence in me, and their confidence is what pushed me to succeed. Looking back, I wonder if I could have accomplished more if I had believed in myself as much as others believed in me.

Dr. Casiero will always be Deena to me, not because I am not proud of her accomplishments and recognize the hard work and dedication it took for her to earn the title of doctor, but because she is like a daughter to me. You can always count on us to find a few moments away from the others at a family gathering to talk about our careers. Even though one may assume I have been the mentor to Deena, she has also mentored me. I am incredibly blessed to have her in my life. To say I have learned from her and benefitted from her advice would be an understatement. I cannot wait to see where she grows from here.

TAKEAWAYS

The chapter offers a deep insight into the life and career journey of Dr. Deena Casiero, touching on various themes such as resilience, determination, breaking barriers, mentorship, leadership, and handling challenges, including imposter syndrome and gender discrimination.

1. **The Role of Family and Mentors**: Your environment, be it family or mentors, plays a significant role in shaping your ambitions and helping you achieve them. Deena's family, as well as mentors like Dr. Hainline and Dr. Anderson, provided the necessary support and guidance for her to rise in her profession.

2. **Resilience Amidst Adversity**: Challenges, both personal and professional, are inevitable. Deena faced them head-on, whether it was personal losses or barriers in her career. Her spirit of resilience is a testament to her character and strength.

3. **The Drive to Break Barriers**: Despite being in a male-dominated industry, Deena's determination to excel and break the glass ceiling showcases the importance of self-belief and the drive to make a mark.

4. **Recognition of Self-worth and Battling Imposter Syndrome**: Many accomplished professionals face imposter syndrome. Acknowledging and working to overcome it, as Deena did, is vital for personal and professional growth.

5. **Grace Under Pressure**: Handling the challenges of the COVID-19 pandemic showcased Deena's leadership skills, ability to innovate, and dedication to ensuring the

safety and well-being of the athletes.

6. **Empowerment and Responsibility**: As a leader, Deena recognized the unique challenges faced by women in her field and took proactive steps to support and empower them. This underlines the importance of leaders being aware and inclusive.

7. **Continuous Learning and Growth**: From her journey from an athletic trainer to the director of sports medicine, Deena's story stresses the importance of continuous learning, adaptability, and seeking out opportunities for growth.

8. **Speaking Up Against Discrimination**: Deena's experience with gender discrimination highlights the gender biases women often face. Her courage in questioning the decision and standing up for her rights serves as a lesson for many not to accept discrimination silently.

These lessons provide insight into Dr. Deena Casiero's journey and offer inspiration and guidance for anyone looking to excel in their respective fields, navigate challenges, and make a lasting impact.

REFLECTIONS

"I never dreamed about success. I worked for it."

Estée Lauder

Chapter Seven

From Entry Level to Corporate Leadership

Crafting a Path to Success

In chapter five, you learned how to have confidence in your abilities. In this chapter, you will learn how to ensure others have confidence in you.

One of my most incredible mentors, both in life and career, once said, "Stay close to the money and be good at it." At the time, he was a vice president for Clear Channel, and I was a sales manager. I had watched him grow his career in entertainment from an entry-level position to the corporate office of a large organization. Therefore, I trusted his advice, and his words resonated with me throughout my career and eventually in my first position as a vice president of sales & marketing over a portfolio of hotels. To this day, I still reflect on the meaning of that statement and have also found it helpful when mentoring others.

The comment was especially meaningful to me because I was in sales. Anyone who has ever been in sales knows that you are only as good as last week's numbers. Literally, no one cares what you did last year. A new year and new goals create a need for someone in sales to drive results week after week. Too many weeks without results would typically end up in termination. At least, that is how I cut my teeth in sales.

One could easily replace "money" with "results," "profit," "company goals," etc. What the phrase really says is to show them your value. In my case, my friend knew I was responsible for driving top-line revenue, so he said, "money." I realized all these years later that he was saying to find what you are good at, hone those skills, and deliver on the company's goals, and you will advance. Great advice! Dumbing it down makes it sound simple, but it is not always easy to navigate.

I am delighted with where I am in my career today. That said, I could have been much further along or had more money in the bank than I do. While I am driven and have a strong work ethic, I have never been good at politics. My direct and outspoken characteristics may not have served me as well as I thought they did when I was younger. Over time, I improved my communication, embracing the philosophy that it is not always what you say but how you say it.

Early in my career, I was the director of catering and convention services and reported to a director of sales and marketing who had his eyes set on a corporate position. He was delighted that in a very short time with the company, people in the corporate office asked about the new director on his team. My talent and skills were being socialized to his bosses. It made him look good because, of course, he hired me.

As time passed, our hotel was asked to host a large corporate event for the executive office. I was asked to attend a planning session for the meeting. In the interest of ensuring the event went off without a hitch, I was vocal about some points made by some of the more senior people at the table and questioned their plan. That said, I was respectful with my communication. Later, back at the hotel, my boss told me I needed to be cautious about challenging plans when they were coming from higher-ups; that could deter me if I ever wanted to move up in the organization. I replied, "If not speaking up and going along with something I don't believe is right or the best solution is the only way for me to grow in this company, then this is not the company for me."

Years later, I would prove I was right, and he was not. The corporate team welcomed my voice from a position of knowledge and professionalism. It resulted in recognition by people who could control my destiny and growth within the company. That company and the people I interacted with there would become the launching pad for my seat in the corporate office.

The director of sales and marketing worked his way up to a vice president position, but even though he was very good at his craft, he chose to take the politically correct "network with the boy's club" route to support his growth. He also forgot where he came from. Practices he would never have allowed from the team he led when we worked together became the norm for him. Apparently, he thought the rules did not apply at a certain level, but he would soon learn how wrong that was.

I do not relish his demise, but I do want to make a critical point for you as the reader. Never forget where you came from. As a leader, you must meet your team where they are. If you are arrogant or, as my daddy would say, "start to believe your own advertisement," it will cause your fall from grace. People will resent you instead of trusting you. Remember, being a vice president or corporate leader does not give you carte blanche to break the rules. Companies have policies for a reason; adhere to them.

Networking is important, but it has its limitations. Don't promise more than you can deliver. Promote yourself from a platform of skill and impact versus "who you know." If you secure your position on the coattail of another, your power will immediately be diminished when they leave. It is essential to promote yourself. I have seen too many people get downsized because they did not promote their value within the company. Once they were gone and it was too late, people were shocked at the number of duties they performed.

I participated in business development presentations with a company I worked for previously. In participating, I witnessed the company's president exaggerate (AKA, lie about) answers to many of the questions asked by the potential client. Leaving a presentation one day, he said, "I've never told a lie I didn't expect to come true one day." When I told my dad about this experience, he said, "Someone who will lie in front of you will lie to you." That proved to be true. Be honest! Honesty is not only an essential attribute as a leader; it should be at the top of your morals list. It is always a good practice to associate yourself with companies and people with moral values and business practices you can align with. If the company has a poor reputation, it will also affect what other companies and recruiters assume about your values.

Early in my career, I had a boss who, whenever I came to him with a problem, would ask, "What is your solution?" It did not take me long to realize that with every problem, I needed to have a solution. This approach to problem-solving will win you many accolades from your boss. On any given day, you are not the only manager bringing an issue to your boss, but if you bring the solution along with the problem, you will rise to the top when your boss thinks about the bench strength of their team.

Don't be a complainer; every problem has a solution. Be the person with a positive attitude in the most adverse situation. Every day will not result in accomplishments and wins for the company. On the days when the company encounters a problem or setback, be a cheerleader, not a whiner.

Be respectful of your boss's time. If you are busy, assume they are even busier. On the other hand, don't assume they are too busy for you to ask for advice. You may not interact much with your boss if you are great at your job. Do not view this as a negative. Your boss may have other more pressing issues needing their attention. That said, don't let too much time go by without ensuring you have one-on-one communication. The best way to do this is by soliciting their opinion and asking for advice on decisions you make on the company's behalf. Come prepared for every conversation to ensure your meeting runs efficiently, for your time and theirs. They will appreciate your approach to collaboration.

Grow where you are planted. Give your company 110%; my mother always taught me that. Come into every day with a good work ethic. Be authentic. If you are not, people will notice. Lack of trust will influence the level of confidence they place in you. Be great at what you do and deliver results consistently. As your industry or position changes due to outlying circumstances like technology, artificial intelligence, customer demand, and workforce, it is essential to stay relevant. The definition of crazy is doing what you have always done and expecting to get the same results. If you are not staying on top of trends and continuing to learn, you may become stale and less impactful to the organization's results.

As you envision your pinnacle of success, it will be important to understand and accept there will be a journey. Big positions come with big responsibilities. When you get there, you must be prepared with knowledge and hands-on experience to ensure you stay there. Treat your ultimate career goal like any other goal. Break it down into smaller goals. My path within the sales and marketing discipline started at an entry-level position. By the time I was a corporate leader, I had covered every position within the sales and marketing department. This meant I had an excellent understanding of the skill sets needed to do the job. My experience ensured I could properly mentor the property-level team.

Depending on where you are currently in your career, you may have several stops on your path before reaching your ultimate goal. Building the experience along the way will make you a stronger leader when you get there and provide a stable foundation for success. Be patient, diligent, and ready to be awesome when you get there.

TAKEAWAYS

1. **Value and Impact Over Visibility**: The advice "Stay close to the money and be good at it" underscores the importance of aligning your skills with the organization's financial goals. This lesson teaches us that true professional value is derived from the impact you make rather than merely being visible in the organization. To progress, we must focus on honing skills that contribute directly to the company's objectives and demonstrate measurable results consistently. It's not about being in the spotlight; it's about making sure your work contributes directly to the organization's success.

2. **Continuous Performance is Key**: Sales is a field where past success is quickly forgotten, and ongoing performance is essential. This principle applies broadly: to progress in any field, you must deliver results consistently. It's a reminder that resting on your laurels is not an option; instead, you must continually strive to achieve and exceed targets to maintain and advance your position.

3. **Authentic Communication Fosters Trust**: Learning how to communicate effectively, especially as you climb the corporate ladder, is crucial. Being direct and outspoken may seem advantageous, but it's also important to be tactful. The way you express your thoughts can either build or erode trust. Authentic, respectful communication is key to being seen as a leader who can handle responsibility at higher levels.

4. **Your Voice Matters**: Speaking up with knowledge and professionalism can lead to recognition and advancement. It's essential to convey your insights and suggestions constructively, even when they challenge the status

quo. This approach not only fosters innovation but can also set you apart as someone ready for leadership, capable of contributing to the organization's strategic direction.

5. **Never Forget Your Roots**: The downfall of the vice president of sales and marketing serves as a cautionary tale about the dangers of arrogance and forgetting one's origins. Staying grounded and maintaining the same principles that guided your early career decisions is critical for long-term success and respect within an organization. Remembering where you came from ensures that you lead with empathy and maintain policies that foster a trustworthy and ethical workplace culture.

6. **Promote Your Value, Not Your Connections**: Networking has its place, but it should never replace genuine skill and impact. Relying on connections rather than competence can be a precarious foundation for a career. It's vital to make sure that others are aware of your contributions and value, as it ensures stability and respect within the company, independent of any single relationship or endorsement.

7. **Honesty Builds Lasting Careers**: Aligning with people and organizations that share your moral values is imperative. Honesty and integrity should be at the core of your professional life. Working with individuals or companies that lack these can not only impede your personal growth but can also tarnish your reputation by association.

8. **Problem-Solving with Solutions in Mind**: Approaching problems with solutions in hand will distinguish you as a proactive and valuable team member. Leaders are inundated with issues; being the person who consistently brings solutions rather than just problems can mark you

as an indispensable asset and place you on the fast track for advancement within the organization.

Each of these lessons serves as a building block for creating a robust career path that is both sustainable and progressive, emphasizing the importance of results, communication, authenticity, remembrance of one's roots, the value of individual contribution over connections, integrity, proactive problem-solving, and consistent performance.

REFLECTIONS

"Girls should never be afraid to be smart."
Emma Watson

CHAPTER EIGHT

Illuminating the Path

The Transformative Power of Mentorship

This book would not be complete without acknowledging the impact mentorship had on me personally and my career growth in hospitality.

The journey of professional growth is like navigating a complex labyrinth. At every turn, one encounters new challenges and opportunities, making the path to success both exhilarating and daunting. In such a journey, the role of a mentor becomes invaluable. A mentor is not just a guide; they are a beacon of wisdom, experience, and insight, illuminating the path ahead with clarity and purpose. Their guidance is a compass that helps steer your career in the right direction, ensuring that every step taken is a step closer to your ultimate goal.

The importance of mentorship cannot be overstated. In a world that's constantly evolving, where new technologies and methodologies are reshaping industries, the guidance of someone who has navigated similar paths is irreplaceable. A mentor provides more than just advice; they offer a perspective that is honed by experience, a nuanced understanding of the industry, and a network of connections that can open doors that might otherwise remain closed. They are a sounding board for ideas, a critic of plans, and a supporter of ambitions. An outstanding mentor communicates with the intention of motivating the listener towards excellence while ensuring not to undermine or destroy their confidence.

Let's continue to explore the profound impact that mentorship can have on your professional journey. Whether you are just starting out, looking to ascend to new heights in your career, or are at the peak of your professional life, the insights and experiences shared here will underscore the transformative power of mentorship. The journey to success is rarely a solitary one – it is often the wisdom and support of a mentor that catalyzes one's growth and propels them towards their aspirations.

The professional networking and guidance a great mentor provides are essential at any stage of your career, especially if you are interested in growing within a large organization or specific industry. Someone who sees your potential and can be brutally honest with you about the areas where you need to improve and develop can be so impactful to your success.

If you do not currently have a person like this in your life, do not be shy about approaching someone who has blazed the path you desire or is in the position you would like. Ask them if they would consider talking to you and providing advice and direction to help you navigate the industry or company where you would like to grow. We often think accomplished people are too busy, but remember they had someone help them, and most people are honored to pay it forward. Just be mindful that they are likely in a demanding position; therefore, come prepared to make the time efficient for both parties. We will discuss this more in-depth in chapter 13, Building Your Personal Board of Directors.

In addition to seeking mentors, it's crucial to be proactive in your professional development. Attend workshops, seminars, and conferences in your industry. These events not only provide valuable knowledge but also offer opportunities to meet potential mentors and peers who share your interests and goals. Engaging in continuous learning shows your mentor that you are serious about your career and willing to invest time and effort into your growth. You should also consider hiring a professional business coach as they can help you understand the best path for your career and help you navigate in a corporate environment.

Networking plays a significant role in finding mentors and advancing your career. Don't limit your networking to formal events; social media platforms like LinkedIn can be powerful tools for connecting with industry leaders. Join groups related to your field, participate in discussions, and don't hesitate to reach out to professionals you admire. Remember, networking is about building genuine relationships. A relationship is a two-way street, so focus on how you can add value to others' professional lives as well.

Lastly, don't overlook the value of peer-to-peer mentorship. Colleagues at a similar stage in their careers can offer unique perspectives, and you can support one another. You understand each other's challenges and can provide relevant advice and encouragement. Peer-to-peer mentorship can evolve into long-term professional relationships that benefit all parties involved.

By embracing these strategies, you enrich your journey towards professional excellence. Always remember, the path to success is not solitary; it's paved with the wisdom and support of those who have walked it before.

If you are someone who has reached the pinnacle of your career, I strongly encourage you to become a mentor to others. More than ever, the young men and women entering the workforce today could benefit from your experience and expertise. You will find it very rewarding to be part of helping someone else achieve their career goals.

As you march forward to a place, purpose, and destiny, and as the pressures of the tasks begin to weigh on your heart, be grateful that God will place people around you who will pray and intercede on your behalf so that you may have the strength to finish strong.

TAKEAWAYS

1. **The Role of a Mentor**: Understand the crucial role mentors play in guiding and illuminating your professional journey. They offer wisdom, experience, and insight, acting as a compass in your career.

2. **The Value of Experienced Guidance**: Recognize the irreplaceable value of having someone who has navigated similar paths in an ever-evolving world. Mentors provide not just advice but a seasoned perspective, industry understanding, and valuable connections.

3. **Effective Communication by Mentors**: Appreciate the importance of how mentors communicate, focusing on motivating and inspiring while maintaining the mentee's confidence.

4. **The Need for Proactivity in Professional Development**: Emphasize the necessity of being proactive in your own growth. This includes attending workshops and seminars, and engaging in continuous learning to show commitment to your career development.

5. **Networking and Relationship Building**: Acknowledge the significance of networking in finding mentors and advancing your career. Utilize various platforms, including social media, and focus on building genuine relationships.

6. **Peer-to-Peer Mentorship**: Recognize the value of mentorship from peers. Colleagues at similar career stages can provide relatable advice and support, and evolve into long-term professional relationships.

7. **Becoming a Mentor**: If you are at the peak of your career, consider becoming a mentor. Sharing your experience and expertise can be rewarding and beneficial to the next generation of professionals.

8. **Spiritual and Emotional Support**: Acknowledge the importance of having people who provide spiritual and emotional support, especially when facing the pressures of your career. This

support can be vital in maintaining strength and focus on your goals.

These lessons underscore the transformative power of mentorship in professional growth, whether one is starting out, scaling new heights, or at the peak of their career.

REFLECTIONS

"Gratitude can transform common days into thanks-givings, turn routine jobs into joy, and change ordinary opportunities into blessings."

William Arthur Ward

CHAPTER NINE

Harnessing the Power of Thought

Learn to Recognize the Landmines: You Are in Control

I t is easier to control your body than your thoughts. However, our thoughts are essential to how we feel, our success, and how others see us. Have you ever wondered why these random thoughts come into your head? Sometimes, my thoughts surprise me, and some thoughts I would never share.

Think about when you are driving in your car alone. You automatically think of staying in the lane, the route to get where you are going, using your turn signal, and all the things that come with operating a car. You may also be listening to the radio or a podcast. Amidst all that, your brain is functioning so highly that you simultaneously have other thoughts popping in and out of your head.

Have you ever tried to meditate and completely close off your thoughts? I find that very difficult. I envy people who can really get into a deep meditative state. I have tried everything – from having one vision of focus that I can return to when my mind starts to wander to seeing those thoughts and envisioning them popping like bubbles. Still, reigning in the constant news feed of my mind remains a formidable task, driven by the power of my brain.

Why is it so important to control your thoughts? Your thoughts are what shape your vision of you. Let's go back to our car ride: you see a woman walking down the sidewalk. She has a lovely physique and is very well-proportioned. Your mind's response to seeing her may be, "I need to lose 10 pounds... I must start working out... why did I inherit my mother's genes?" All those thoughts make you feel inferior to the woman walking down the street. You begin to develop a vision of yourself that is dissatisfied with your physical appearance. This is a confidence killer, for sure!

Let's continue our journey. A song on the radio reminds you of a friend or companion. Perhaps this relationship did not end well, and you are reminded of the breakup and the feeling of abandonment. You find yourself thinking of everything you could or should have done differently. Yet, snap back to the present; you have long moved past this time in your life. You may or may not be in a new relationship, but let's assume you made peace with it a while ago. These random thoughts of the past are causing you to second-guess yourself and relive memories that did not give you joy then and are certainly not making you feel good now.

Sometimes, these random thoughts come from the voices in our head, the voices of others that have now become an inner voice in our head. Have you ever had a personal goal? Maybe you wanted to start a business, get in shape, write a book, climb a mountain – it could be any number of things. There is one thing you can always count on: when you start telling people your plan, at least one person (maybe more) will tell you why you can't do it. Everyone has what I call "dream smashers" in their life who will give them a hundred reasons why they cannot accomplish their dreams. They are loud, and their voices are lasting. It is like they set up residence in our heads, and every time we start executing our plan, we hear them saying, "You can't." It is hard enough to accomplish your goals with all the other things life is throwing at you. The last thing you need is a dream smasher babbling in your ear. Focus on the voices saying, "You've got this!" "Yes, you can!" "You can do anything you set your mind to." Train your thoughts to be positive affirmations. You can also encourage yourself by recognizing the negative thoughts and turning them into positive affirmations.

So, how do we stop these thoughts from constantly coming at us? I am not sure you can stop them, but you can control them. I have adapted the advice of Dr. Wayne Dyer as written in his book, *Wishes Fulfilled*. Dr. Dyer relates these thoughts to the ticker tape of the stock exchange and how it feels like never-ending thoughts scrolling through your mind at any given time.[17] I have adapted the practice he taught. As these thoughts come into your mind, spend a few seconds thinking about how each thought makes you feel. Does it make you feel good, loved, at peace, strong, and successful? Or does it make you feel sad, afraid, not good enough, and insecure? Depending on my mind's response to the thought, I envision myself either flicking it away into the abyss or tucking it into my heart. That is the practice I have adapted to control my thoughts.

It is still easier to practice a 90-minute hot yoga class in a 106-degree room with 40% humidity than to consistently control my thoughts, but as they say, "practice makes perfect" (pun intended). Having a practice to address them and understand how they make me feel has undoubtedly increased my self-confidence and determination to accomplish my goals.

One last thought: this practice of controlling your thoughts needs to come naturally in your work environment. To manage your thoughts naturally at work, it needs to become a practice you embody 24/7, and the development of the practice should start in your personal environment where you are more at ease and able to be yourself without the judgment, distraction, and interference of others.

I believe that when you say I am, what comes next is being spoken into existence. You are putting it out into the universe. I have a practice of "I am" meditation. I am sharing mine as an example, but I encourage you to develop your own.

Lovell's ABCs of Affirmations

I am abundant.	I am necessary.
I am blessed.	I am obedient.
I am cared for.	I am persistent
I am determined.	I am qualified.
I am enough.	I am resilient.
I am faithful.	I am satisfied.
I am grateful.	I am truthful.
I am happy.	I am unstoppable.
I am intuitive.	I am valued.
I am joyful.	I am wise.
I am kind.	I am extra special in God's eyes.
I am loved.	I am young at heart.
I am meek.	I am zin.

Exodus 3:14 – God said to Moses, "I am who I am. This is what you are to say to the Israelites: I am has sent me to you."

******

"I've learned that people will forget what you said, people will forget what you did, but people will never forget how you made them feel."

Maya Angelou

It would be easy to go through life feeling good about yourself and living in this realm of peace, love, and happiness if all you had to do was learn to control your thoughts and respond to them appropriately. However, as human beings, we do not live in a solitary world; therefore, we constantly encounter other human beings. At every encounter with another human, you are subject to the emotional baggage the other person carries. This emotional baggage may come from conditioning experienced in their forma-tive years and never recognized or addressed, even as adults.

One of my fellow yogis is an amazing, always positive woman. I have never encountered her where I did not leave uplifted and feeling better about myself, life's circumstances, and spiritually stronger. Her positivity and joy are infectious! She is the opposite of Debbie Downer, and I light up when I see her in class. I know that she has faced loss and challenges in life, but somehow, she did not let it leave her embittered. Instead, she seems to have grown stronger from the lessons learned in these situations. I know I am better for knowing her and that, without fail, I will go away feeling uplifted from my encounter with Sherri.

Unfortunately, not everyone has the demeanor of my friend, and too often, you can leave an encounter with others feeling worse than before you met up. Negativity is like a wet blanket; most of the time, the person emitting the negative has become very comfortable wallowing in self-pity. Debbie Downer can wreak havoc on your good mood, and if you stick around long enough, you'll find yourself sharing her wet blanket. This behavior can be especially prevalent in a corporate environment. Let's be honest! On any given day, we can find something to complain about: our boss, colleagues, process, culture, clients...I could go on because the list is long.

I have been the person creating the drama, I have been the victim of the drama (the one people complained about), and I am often the person that people vent to when the drama is overwhelming for them. In all three of these scenarios, you need to "nip drama in the bud."

Complaining creates drama. Instead of complaining about an issue, spend that same energy figuring out how you would solve the situation and apply a solution.

If you have been leading for any length of time, you will find yourself in a situation where someone registers a complaint to your direct report or the human resources department. There are one of two solutions in this case: own it or defend it.

Owning it – Sometimes, even the best leaders have a bad day or make mistakes. You may have taken your lousy day or emotions out on your team member, and in that case, you need to say, "Point taken. Is there anything I need to do to make amends?" Then, you need to learn from that experience and avoid that behavior in the future.

There will be situations where managers and associates will defend their mistakes by making you the scapegoat, which can create liability for you and your company, especially if the associate's goal is a lawsuit. It is always important to document your conversations with your direct reports, and in the case of performance improvement, when you have the documentation, defending your position in the situation is a more efficient process.

As a leader, you must be available as a sounding board. People need to vent and blow off steam, and you need to allow them that space. My team members know they can call me and "call a vent session." I will be in listening mode, letting them get it off their heart and mind. There are two scenarios where your team may break out in a venting session:

One is what I refer to as the safe place vent. They have built trust with you as their leader and know they can call a vent session about any situation in a no-judgment zone. In this case, you listen and do not even try to respond until they have exhausted themselves. You will find that a one-way conversation burns out quickly. After they are done, you can mentor them and give them options on handling the situation – again, with compassion, not judgment. This approach is vital in this scenario, or they will lose trust and feel uncomfortable calling you when the next situation presents itself.

The second scenario may occur when you are in the middle of meeting a deadline, completing a project, or in a group meeting. The initiative's outcome could suffer if you allow the rant to go on for too long. Depending on the situation, you need to determine an internal timer of how long you will let the venting session go on without dialing it back and resuming the task. Every situation will create a unique approach, and this is when you must lean into your experience and attributes as a leader. In those instances, I will call a time out, remind them we have a goal to accomplish, acknowledge I have allowed them to be heard, and provide an opportunity to follow up if the circumstances require additional follow-up.

The landmines in the workplace can be many. How you respond is important. The "knee-jerk" approach can create additional issues and, in most cases, never brings a solution. We have all been there when a situation makes us angry, and we react with the first thing that comes to mind. That is never a good practice. In these situations, I recommend a pause, take a breath, and let the news you are receiving settle in for a moment or more. It is also important to ask questions instead of immediately responding with comments and opinions. Make sure you get the whole story and not just one side. I have experienced leaders who would react to a situation based on the first version they received. The first version is not always the full version and is based on timing, not necessarily the accuracy of the situation.

The best leaders are the ones who solicit more information before developing and imposing a strong opinion about the person or situation being discussed. My mother has always said, "There are three sides to every situation: your side, their side, and the right side." It is never fun to admit you were wrong, and without all the information, you are in jeopardy of making poor decisions that could hurt others or inhibit the team's success.

Recently, I was on a plane talking to the passenger next to me; we discussed the analogy of the glass half full versus the glass half empty. I loved his view! He said, "I always come to a situation with my glass full," and pointed out, "Even if the liquid only fills the glass to the halfway point, there is still something there, gases or air." Consider this view when faced with landmines in the workplace; it will be essential to come "full" of knowledge, information, and experience to navigate around them.

TAKEAWAYS

1. **The Importance of Thought Awareness**: Understanding the power of thoughts is crucial, as they significantly influence our emotions, behaviors, and how we view ourselves and the world around us. Like unsuspected landmines, certain thoughts can detonate negative feelings and self-perceptions. By learning to recognize these harmful patterns, we begin the journey of mastering our internal narrative. Recognizing that we can't always control the appearance of random thoughts, but we can choose which to engage with, empowers us to maintain a healthier mental environment.

2. **The Difficulty of Thought Control**: Controlling our thoughts, especially during tasks that require less conscious thought, like driving, can be remarkably challenging. While our brains manage routine actions almost automatically, they also generate a constant stream of consciousness that includes random and sometimes unwanted thoughts. The endeavor to meditate and quiet the mind illustrates the difficulty of achieving a still mind, demonstrating the persistent and invasive nature of thoughts. Yet, acknowledging this difficulty is the first step towards developing strategies for better thought management.

3. **The Impact of Comparisons**: When we engage in comparisons, particularly those that judge our worth or appearance against others, we often emerge feeling inadequate. These automatic self-assessments can lead to a diminished self-image and erode confidence. It's vital to recognize these thought patterns as detrimental and consciously redirect our thoughts towards self-acceptance and positive self-affirmation. Acknowledging that such

comparisons are often unfair and unproductive can help us foster a more positive self-view.

4. **The Weight of the Past Can Be Heavy**: Thoughts of past experiences, especially unresolved or painful ones, can easily disrupt our present well-being. They can cause us to question our decisions, leading to unnecessary self-doubt and regret. It's important to consciously acknowledge these thoughts as echoes of the past that do not need to define our current reality. By focusing on the present and cultivating a practice of letting go, we can avoid the emotional pitfalls these memories may present.

5. **Counter Negative Voices**: Throughout our lives, we encounter "dream smashers," individuals who cast doubt on our ambitions and abilities. Their negative voices can linger in our minds, undermining our self-belief and motivation. To combat this, we must consciously amplify the positive voices, including our own, and affirm our capabilities and worth. By consistently countering the negative with positive affirmations, we build resilience against external skepticism and internal self-doubt.

6. **Manage Intrusive Thoughts**: Since it is not always possible to stop intrusive thoughts from entering our minds, developing a method to manage them is essential. By evaluating how each thought affects our emotional state, we can decide which to discard and which to embrace. The practice of mentally "flicking away" negative thoughts or "tucking" positive ones into our hearts can be a useful technique. Such practices help us cultivate a mental environment that promotes peace and positivity.

7. **The Practice of Control**: Like any skill, thought control requires consistent practice and dedication. Implement-

ing regular practices such as mindfulness, meditation, or yoga can provide a framework for managing thoughts. By doing so, we can improve our mental discipline, increase our self-confidence, and strengthen our resolve to achieve personal goals. The adage "practice makes perfect" aptly applies to the realm of thought control, emphasizing the value of persistent effort.

8. **Affirmations in Personal and Professional Life**: Integrating positive affirmations into our daily routines is beneficial both personally and professionally. By beginning in a personal, judgment-free space, the practice can become a natural part of our mindset, eventually permeating professional interactions and environments. Affirmations such as my ABCs serve as powerful tools to manifest positivity and self-belief, reinforcing the idea that the words following "I am" have the power to shape reality and should be chosen with intention and care.

These lessons emphasize the significance of controlling your thoughts, fostering positivity, and using thought management as a tool for personal and professional growth. Additionally, they highlight the importance of empathy and effective communication in navigating challenges and conflicts in the workplace.

REFLECTIONS

"The only limit to our realization of tomorrow will be our doubts of today."

Franklin D. Roosevelt

CHAPTER TEN

Strength of Body and Spirit

Erika McKee, Certified Personal Trainer, Empower Fitness

W hen I first had the idea to include the stories of women in this book, I was focused on highly accomplished women with success stories. Telling the story of how they reached the pinnacle of their career was what I was going for; however, when I met Erika McKee, that all changed. I realized that the journey of a woman takes many paths in life. Every story has a beginning, and somewhere woven into the story is the birth of the drive and determination to change your circumstances. There is a pivotal moment where you find the courage to stop waiting and start achieving your personal goals. When Erika started refusing to let others dictate her future, that is when she began to bloom.

I first met Erika when she was weeks away from leaving her marital home of 20+ years. It was a brief meeting; my husband and I were considering her to replace our housekeeper, and she came to tour our home and discuss expectations. She mentioned she was moving into our neighborhood, and she and her daughter could help us with pet sitting or walking our dogs. While I did not know Erika personally, she had come recommended by our previous friend and housekeeper.

Some time went by, and I asked my husband if he had heard from Erika about cleaning. He texted her, and she said she would not be able to clean our house. Since she had never professionally cleaned houses, she was afraid she would disappoint. I found that odd but assumed she had just changed her mind. She did offer pet sitting and mentioned she was a personal trainer in the event we or anyone we knew would be interested.

A few weeks went by, and I really did not think much more about Erika; I just figured I would see her around the neighborhood. The next few weeks for me consisted of much travel, both international and domestic. The long flights and too much sitting landed me in the emergency room with back spasms that I compared to childbirth. I was in so much pain that I thought for sure I was headed for the operating room. However, the young doctor simply said, "You have nothing wrong with your spine, but if you do not want to end up here every three months getting steroids and muscle relaxers, I suggest you work on your core."

Thus begins my relationship with Erika. Never wanting to feel the excruciating pain of back spasms again for the rest of my life, I signed up for two personal training sessions a week. My first impression of Erika was her sweet and caring spirit. She was born to be a personal trainer because she genuinely cared about making people stronger – not just physically, but the whole package of mind, body, and spirit. At the first session, Erika had no clue about my background, so I simply smiled when she asked if I had a problem with her playing praise music while we worked out. Her faith and trust in God were evident. It almost seemed she was holding on to God a little tighter than the norm. I would soon learn why.

At each session, Erika would show up to help me strengthen my muscles, and I learned she was also put in my life for another reason. It was meant for me to help her become stronger in many other ways. You see, because of challenges in her personal life, she had reached a point where she was looking for a more peaceful life for herself and her family. Her strength and confidence to carry on and move forward were driven by her commitment to providing her four children, ages six to 16, with a safe and happy environment.

At every training session, Erika and I became closer, and she started to share information with me about her situation and her childhood. Her mother died after a long battle with cancer before Erika was married. Her only parenting was the tough love of her father. In the first few months of her marriage separation, the struggles were great, mentally, physically, and financially. Watching Erika's journey in those first few months was very familiar for me as I, too, faced a similar experience in my first marriage and the separation that followed.

Sometimes, you need a reason to fight for better, and since all Erika ever wanted to do was be a wife and mother, her children became the foundation for her drive. She had to take care of her family. Her second passion is her love for physical fitness and helping others become stronger, and Erika is fantastic at training. After several months of odd jobs that included home health care and pet sitting, Erika began to consider the possibility of starting her own business. She had clients for some time that she trained, but it was part-time and just extra money. It was never her sole source of income.

The strength training sessions became a dual session of Erika training me and me providing her the life coaching she needed in her circumstances. In the very beginning, the best thing Erika had going for her was her unwavering faith in God. It sustained her throughout the marriage, and she was clinging to His word as she faced one of the biggest storms of her life.

It did not take me long to realize how little confidence she had in her own abilities. She also found it difficult to advocate for herself. Even setting prices for her training, she devalued her worth, thinking people would not feel she was worth the fee. 20+ years of conditioning caused Erika to avoid confrontation by giving in. Instead of saying no, she took the route of peacemaker to avoid the alternative.

This type of conditioning is not something that corrects itself just by leaving the environment where it existed. The longer a person is exposed to the conditioning, the longer the recovery. However, Erika was willing to be coached and do the work required to improve the future for herself and her children.

Like many young entrepreneurs, Erika lacked the marketing and administrative skills to grow a successful business. However, learning how to do these tasks was not an obstacle because she had the intelligence. Time management was the real culprit. Erika needed to find a balance between her motherly duties, the other odd jobs outside of personal training, and her inability to say no. She needed to realize what was the highest priority and best use of her time because, in a personal training business, time is money.

Most small business owners are good at the service they provide, but many fail due to the absence of processes for the financial and legal requirements to be profitable. Additionally, branding and marketing are needed to provide a pipeline of customers to sustain and support the growth of the company.

In my job as an SVP of commercial strategies, I am protected by the systems my company has in place for human resources, finance, and business development. There is comfort in knowing I have benefits and a reliable income stream. A small business owner cannot take these for granted, and without these systems, the business may fail or, at the very least, not reach the full potential of profitability.

Fortunately, Erika embraced the life coaching I was providing her. I continued to hold her ultimate vision in front of her, helping her recognize that she needed to set small goals to achieve the greater vision. I was so proud of her as I began to witness the evolution of her emotional healing, which had to come first. The way she set the priorities of "family first" ensured her children also experienced a healthy transition to this new way of life. As all of this began to settle, I started to see green shoots of self-confidence, resilience, and strength that she did not possess when I first met her.

I have often said, "Knowing the problem exists places you halfway to the solution." Erika was a perfect example of this. She was willing to recognize her weaknesses to address them and overcome them. So often, people are not able to change their thoughts and behavior because they do not take the time to perform a self-diagnosis and act on the things they need to work on or change.

Today, Erika is the sole proprietor of Empower Fitness, a small business providing personal training to individuals as well as local gyms and wellness offices. While it is still in the startup phase, the company and Erika are thriving. Exchanging strength for strength at each session, Erika and I became two women supporting each other to their fullest potential: physically for me and mentally for her.

Even through the darkest moments, Erika never lost faith or forgot to give God praise for bringing her through another day. I know that there will be even bigger successes for Erika in the future, and her unwavering faith and determination will take her there.

If you feel stuck in a relationship or work environment where you are not thriving as a person or professional, the first step to a new life may be out of the door of the old one. For six years, I ran two marathons each year. If you have ever run a marathon, you know that the most challenging part is the training, not the actual marathon. On training days, I would have an 18- or 20-mile training run, and the hardest step of the morning was the one I took out of my front door. When I stopped listening to the excuses in my head and started running, it ended successfully and prepared me to achieve the ultimate goal of finishing the marathon.

As you seek to find your own purpose and achieve your vision, remember the path to success is not a sprint; it is a marathon, and speed should not be the goal but instead finishing strong.

TAKEAWAYS

1. **Shift in Perspective**: The most profound insights often come when we shift our perspective and open ourselves to stories beyond our initial vision. Being receptive to change can lead to deeper understanding and connection.

2. **Strength Beyond Physicality**: While physical strength and wellness are essential, mental and emotional strength are equally crucial. Helping someone improve their physical health can often be intertwined with aiding their mental and emotional well-being.

3. **The Power of Mutual Support**: Genuine relationships are reciprocal. Just as Erika has helped me physically, I know I have played a role in Erika's emotional healing. Through mutual support, we are both growing stronger.

4. **Recognizing Red Flags**: Understanding the signs of a toxic relationship, whether it's with a partner or within a work environment, is crucial. Erika's story underscores the importance of identifying these signs and the bravery required to act on them.

5. **Personal Growth Requires Facing Challenges Head-On**: Erika's willingness to confront and work on her vulnerabilities, rather than ignoring them, paved the way for her growth. Self-awareness and action are key components of personal development.

6. **The Significance of Faith**: Erika's unwavering faith was her anchor through turbulent times. It provided her strength and hope, demonstrating the profound impact spirituality can have on one's resilience and outlook.

7. **Entrepreneurship Beyond Skill**: While a passion or skill might drive an entrepreneur, success often requires a balanced understanding of other aspects like marketing, administration, and self-assertion. Erika's journey into entrepreneurship underscores this multi-faceted approach.

8. **Life as a Marathon**: Life's challenges are not sprints; they require endurance, resilience, and persistence. It's not about the

speed, but the journey and the lessons learned along the way. Facing obstacles and pushing past them, just as in marathon training, is integral to personal growth and achievement.

REFLECTIONS

"Nothing is impossible, the word itself says 'I'm possible'!"

Audrey Hepburn

CHAPTER ELEVEN

Mastering the Art of Interpersonal Dynamics in the Workplace

S tarting a new job is never easy; you spend the first thirty days trying to remember where the extra office supplies are and the names and responsibilities of your coworkers, all while learning your new job. Just as you start to feel like you've got this, you begin to become familiar with the different personalities you are working with. Whoa! No one mentioned these characters when they were selling you on the culture of the company. You know the drill, the constant complainer, the one that never learned to play nice in the sandbox, the one that is trying but failing at keeping up with the Joneses, and let's not forget Mr. or Ms. Know It All. All these individuals come from a place of jealousy and insecurity; they show up every day trying to drag you into their vortex of negativity.

Throughout my career, I have experienced many of these personalities from colleagues. I am also certain that as I was earning my wings as a leader, I was not always an inspiration to others either. My strong, sometimes abrasive, personality could have an adverse effect on those around me. I wince when I recollect the times I made people feel inadequate, self-doubting, or simply miserable.

It took me a long time to realize that I was in the driver's seat in these unfortunate encounters with others. As I reflect on workplace relationships, two examples come to mind. Let's start with the negative example so that we can end this chapter on a positive note.

Some coworkers come with a big personality that can seem a little egotistical. Beware, be very aware of big personalities because, in many cases, they are overcompensating for something else. I can promise you there is nothing more frustrating than someone who acts like a big shot and, all the while, they are feeling insecure and jealous of you. You will become the victim of their imposter syndrome or insecurities. It can result in you becoming a target at every meeting, company gathering, and even private conversation with the boss when you are not there to defend yourself. Additionally, as you begin to catch on to these tactics, they will also be getting to know you and finding ways to "push your buttons" that make you look like the mean girl. They literally study you and learn how to tear you down by making you look like an emotional mess or an unprofessional leader. It is unfortunate that everyone can't just respect each other and get along, but sometimes, that's just not how life works.

The one thing these types of people do not have in their bag of tricks is power over you. No, really, all the ploys in the world, even the successful ones, do not give them the power. You still have the power. You have the power to pause, and you have the power not to react. If they push you to the point of anger, simply walk away. Any reaction will allow them to have power over you at that moment, but if you pause or don't respond, you have retained control of the encounter. Pausing or walking away doesn't mean you will never address the situation, but it will allow for a more thoughtful and less emotional response. Just remember, if you explode or become emotional, you will enable them to push your buttons, and they have accomplished their goals. Retain your power, and sooner than later, you will find you not only have the power, but you also have control.

In my long tenure in a corporate environment, I have also learned that taking time to know what feeds someone's insecurity, abrasive personality, or know-it-all persona is usually born from their conditioning years. Once you understand what is fueling this behavior, it becomes easier to determine how you respond and professionally relate to them. The choices you make in communicating and engaging with this person will bring one of two outcomes: positivity or negativity. I recommend choosing the peaceful route and going for positivity.

I will use myself as an example of how conditioning can be used as an advantage to your leadership style. As previously mentioned, the conditioning from my parents consisted of a mother who said, "Pull your bootstraps up and keep on going," and a father who said, "Walk in that room like you own it." In the early years of my career as a less experienced leader, this conditioning likely created the perception of an arrogant, abrasive bull in a China shop. Trust me, flawed perceptions in a corporate environment can be a career killer. Let's break down the "why" of the advice my parents were giving me.

At 27 years old, my mother became a single parent with custody of two daughters, ages five and seven. To make ends meet, my mom worked four jobs at one time. I can vividly recall my sister and I having to wake her up between her various shifts, sometimes even having to remind her which job she was headed to next. When I was married to the father of my daughter, we only had one car. My mother would pick me up at 5:30 AM to take me to my job as a hostess and server at a local restaurant. She knew that I was facing relationship issues in my marriage, and she would coach me all the way to work, saying, "Leave your troubles at the door and give your boss 110%." In other words, pull your bootstraps up because you have a daughter to take care of, and your problems will still be there when you get home. Understanding the reason, she provided this survival tool, eventually turning the abrasive bull in a China shop into a person who has a very strong work ethic. No one could ever accuse me of stealing time from my employer and not showing up to give 100% every day.

My dad's advice of walking in the room like you own it also

came from his conditioning growing up. I am a preacher's kid, and my grandfather was also a preacher. My grandparents spent over 50 years in the Church of God organization in Cleveland, TN. A legacy that I am very proud of. When my daddy was growing up as a child of a Pentecostal pastor, it was not easy. Daily, my dad and his siblings were ridiculed and made fun of because of their religious beliefs and practices. They were also poor, and my grandparents had ten children. They provided a very strong faith foundation, but preachers then did not make much money and were at the lower end of the economic class. For years, my father suffered from insecurity, and even long after becoming one of the country's top 20 television evangelists, he still had to overcome his insecurity. Recognizing that my dad's advice was born from his own challenges with insecurities led him to teach his children to hold their heads up, throw their shoulders back, and walk in that room like we owned it. It was not to instill arrogance in us but instead to impart a high level of confidence.

Understanding the motives behind a person's actions can help you find a way to be the bigger person and find a commonality that will allow for a positive working relationship. Drama and division will destroy productivity, and then nobody wins. Lastly, holding on to anger, frustration, or complaining does not present the best version of you.

"Dreamweaver Dave" was the opposite of the big shot personality. Dave was the person who showed up every day, recognizing people's strengths and potential. He had a subliminal way of coaching and promoting the people he worked with. Dave was responsible for launching many people's careers, and I was fortunate to cross his path early on. I was always the person who, six months into a role, would set their eyes on the next role. When I first met Dave, he was the president of the company I worked for, and at the time, I was a director of catering. Three years into my tenure with the company, I set my sights on becoming a director of sales & marketing. What I did not know was how much Dave followed my career through conversations and positive endorsements from other executives in the company. One weekend, attending a crab fest, Dave and his wife sat at a table for four with me and my husband. Nothing about the conversation looked or felt like an interview, but apparently, it was because Dave called and offered me my first Director of Sales position the next day. Looking back, I was probably in over my head, but Dave and others continued to support and mentor me to success. For the first few months, without exception, I would get a weekly call, and he would ask me one question, "Are you still having fun?"

I was still working for Dave when I received an offer to take an above-property position responsible for 27 hotels. When news of my resignation was known to Dave, he called me. He did not try to talk me into staying, but he had a very open and honest conversation with me. He advised me on how to succeed at the company I would work for. The comment I will never forget was, "Not many people can go from one hotel to twenty-seven and succeed, but if anyone can, you will." He still supported and encouraged my career goals even though I was leaving his company. Ten years later, when I was leaving that company and starting my consulting firm, Dave was one of the first people I called. He has remained a friend and advisor to this day.

I wholeheartedly urge you to take a moment to acknowledge the young talent around you, those brimming with potential. Never let an opportunity slip by to inspire and advocate for them, even to higher-ups, thus shaping their career trajectories. Depending on where you are in your career, your objectives might currently revolve around job titles and financial gains. However, I assure you that as time passes, these goals will evolve into a focus on the legacy you leave behind—a legacy characterized by mentorship and aiding others in finding their paths to growth and development. The earlier you start this journey, the more fulfilled you'll be with each new day that dawns.

TAKEAWAYS

1. **Navigating Personalities Requires Self-Control**: Starting a new job involves adapting to a variety of personalities that may be challenging. It's important to remember that each person's behavior is often a reflection of their own insecurities. While it's easy to get caught up in the negativity, maintaining self-control is crucial. Reacting in anger or frustration gives difficult coworkers power over you, whereas pausing and walking away keeps you in control and allows you to address the situation more thoughtfully later.

2. **Retaining Power in Conflict**: In confrontations, retaining power is less about authority and more about the ability to remain composed. The real power lies in not allowing others to disrupt your emotional state. By choosing not to react immediately, you preserve your agency and set the terms for any future engagement on your own, more rational grounds. This strategy prevents escalation and keeps you from being manipulated.

3. **Understanding Roots of Behavior Can Guide Interaction**: Recognizing the origins of someone's problematic behavior can provide valuable insights into how to interact with them. People's negative or challenging traits are often products of their past experiences. By understanding these underlying factors, you can communicate more effectively and choose a response that fosters positivity rather than perpetuating negativity.

4. **Leveraging Personal History to Shape Leadership**: Personal history and upbringing can significantly influence one's professional demeanor and leadership style. Reflecting on the advice from influential figures in your

life can help in understanding your actions and perceptions in the workplace. This reflection can lead to a more conscious and deliberate application of such advice, helping transform potential weaknesses into strengths.

5. **Perceptions Can Be Career-Defining**: How others perceive you in the workplace can make or break your career. Early in a professional journey, assertiveness and confidence can be misconstrued as arrogance. It's vital to be aware of these perceptions and work to mitigate any negative impressions by demonstrating a strong work ethic and collaboration.

6. **Every Day is a Chance for a Fresh Start**: Embrace each day as an opportunity for growth and improvement in all roles you play, whether it be as a leader, coworker, or family member. By visualizing every morning as the start of a new chapter, you can focus on bringing the best version of yourself forward, leaving behind any previous day's mistakes or regrets.

7. **Mentorship is Key to Legacy and Fulfillment**: Recognizing and nurturing young talent can have a lasting impact on their careers and your own personal legacy. Acts of mentorship and advocacy are not only beneficial to those you support but are also deeply fulfilling. As you progress in your career, you'll find that helping others achieve their goals becomes a more rewarding objective than personal accolades or financial success.

8. **Encouragement Fosters Success**: Supportive colleagues and mentors, like "Dreamweaver Dave," can have a profound impact on one's career trajectory. Encouragement and belief in someone's potential can motivate and propel them to take on challenges and achieve success. Always

look for opportunities to support and mentor others, as these relationships can become lifelong connections that enrich both professional and personal lives.

This chapter underscores the importance of personal growth, understanding and appreciating the motivations of others, and the value of mentorship in a professional setting.

REFLECTIONS

"The most common way people give up their power is by thinking they don't have any."

Alice Walker

CHAPTER TWELVE

Rising Above the Challenges of Transition

Joy Thrash, President & Founder of Business Resource Management

I want to introduce you to my sister, Joy Thrash. She married her high school sweetheart after graduating high school in 1983. Her son, Christopher, was born two years later; in 1990, her daughter Jessica was born.

Joy's drive to succeed has always been fueled by helping people. Her desire to do that led her to her accomplishments and the work she does today. Joy said, "At each stop in my career, the drive to make a difference for the people prompted me to seek out where I could help in an organization, community, and team." Her career started in banking, but after ten years with Wachovia Bank, she was told she had gone as far as she could go without a degree, even though she was training new associates who had a degree.

As a young wife with two young children, it had to be a daunting decision to go to college. But not willing to settle, Joy began taking classes at the local community college. Fifteen years after graduating high school, she received a bachelor's degree in accounting from Methodist University in Fayetteville, North Carolina, graduating magna cum laude. She also had a 4.0 GPA from Fayetteville Community College.

Joy's tenacity is a shining example to others that you do not have to settle, and better is achievable if you are willing to put in the work. Being a wife and mother raising her children and working full-time wasn't easy. If you want the reward, you must put the work in.

After college, Joy worked in an accounting firm for one year but realized she would prefer to use her skills in finance management for a mid-size company or small business. "Sometimes it is as important to know what you don't want as it is to know what you do want," said Joy.

In 1997, she embarked on a 10-year career with the Chamber of Commerce in Fayetteville, North Carolina. She started as a bookkeeper but would soon become the VP of finance. When the president's position came open, Joy served as the liaison between the staff and the board of directors as they recruited for a new president. It is here that she met Bill Martin, an expert in the field of economic development. When he joined the organization as the president, it was evident he and Joy would work well together. Joy said, "Bill was pivotal to my career; he allowed me to do what I was capable of. I was not a threat to him. He knew I could complement the work he did." This working relationship created success for the Chamber of Commerce, and not only was the organization and community thriving, but so was Joy. Her leadership within the organization expanded across disciplines, and she eventually became the senior vice president, second in charge to the president.

Eight years into Joy's tenure with the Chamber of Commerce, her career was fulfilling, and she was contributing to the organization's and staff's growth. At the time, her role had not only gained her respect as a leader across disciplines, but she had also become a high-profile professional within the local community. Unfortunately, the fulfillment she experienced during her tenure was about to be challenged. Bill Martin left the organization, and business politics took over following his departure.

As they were recruiting for a new president, a local businessman was asked to serve as interim president. You can imagine that, as he was sitting in the chair, Joy was still the one who was executing and keeping the day-to-day operations running smoothly for the team. Finally, a new president was selected, and Joy would soon experience what it was like to report to someone threatened by her experience and position in the organization.

"I was told I had too much power and made too much money as a woman," she explained. "I was also in a combative environment." The new president gave all department managers the title of senior vice president to undermine Joy's authority within the organization. He also left her off the invitation for departmental meetings.

I asked Joy why she stayed in such a toxic environment for two more years. She responded, "I tend to get sucked into thinking I can make a difference and protect the people. That has always been my kryptonite."

After ten years with the Chamber of Commerce, Joy was coming to the realization she was very likely going to be fired. She knew she would need another position, so she began to interview. Joy's role in the community made her very well-known to the local businesses, and upon returning to the office after her first interview, word had already reached the president's office. He called her into his office and informed her he knew she had been interviewed. He said, "When I know people are looking for another job, I let them go."

Getting fired was devastating. Joy had put her heart and soul into this job, which came with community and a work family. With such a high-profile position in the community, it escalated the level of embarrassment. Joy had seen how the "boys' club" worked up close and personal, and her observant nature helped her link the dots. Fortunately, karma is real, and Joy had an opportunity to use one of their mistakes to negotiate a severance that would buy her some time. During the last conversation with the president, he asked her, "What spin would you like to put on this?" Joy replied, "What spin? Anyone who knows me knows this is not what I want."

In the aftermath, Joy realized how well she was respected by the people she impacted in her position. She said, "People who rally around you help you through things like this. I knew I could not let this change me; I had to leave the same person I was when I started with the organization."

You have heard it said when it rains, it pours! If Joy wasn't going through enough professionally, at the same time, her marriage of 35 years ended. Realizing life changes, people can develop differently and move in different directions. Even with this understanding, the divorce was heartbreaking.

The darkest hour of her career would become the brightest light for Joy's success. Sometimes, you do have to have a Judas in your life to help you get to the next place. There are times when the Lord may want to move you, and unless you are shaken to an extent you could never go back, it may prevent you from leaving and, most importantly, moving forward.

Joy's severance ran out, and for the first and only time in her life, she had to apply for unemployment compensation. Before she could collect her third unemployment check, Joy was hired by an organization attempting to start the All-American Defense Business Association as a subsidiary of an existing association. The new association would promote collaboration between local businesses and the military. Within six months, the new organization would become its own entity. As a one-woman show, Joy became the founding director of the North Carolina Defense Business Association (NCDBA).

Joy asked, "Have you ever heard that phrase 'fake it until you make it'? Well, I needed a job, and I was in a position where I just had to figure it out." She went on to say, "Had they told me I would be advocating to support the NCDBA initiatives to the state and federal government, building a membership from ground zero, organizing committees across the state, building an infrastructure for B2B networking, and being a voice for the military across the entire state of North Carolina, I would have said, 'You have the wrong person, I am not qualified to do all that.'" That said, Joy began to eat the elephant one bite at a time. She soon learned that every skill set learned at the Fayetteville Chamber of Commerce was needed to develop and run the NCDBA.

During her time with the chamber, the Military Affairs organization within the chamber needed a revitalization. The person in charge of the department was not prioritizing it, and the members wanted to disengage and start their own organization independent of the Chamber of Commerce.

Our stepfather served in Vietnam and always taught Joy and me to respect the military's men and women and see them as heroes. Joy thought working with the military would be an honor, and she asked Bill Martin to allow her to take over the Military Affairs organization. The relationship was successful, and the organization remained part of the Chamber. Her only regret was that our stepfather, Robert, was not alive to see her interaction with the military and discuss this wonderful experience of service with him.

Seven years later, Joy was no longer faking it but was succeeding at every turn. Her previous work with the military expanded in her new role, and she was able to create a more successful platform for the NCDBA.

The vision and concept she started with became a well-respected statewide organization; membership grew from zero to 250 statewide, and the NCDBA was endorsed by the secretary of the North Carolina Department of Commerce as the defense trade association for North Carolina.

Joy was appointed to the Governors Military Affairs Council; she was the only woman and civilian on the council at the time. A retired general was the council leader, and Joy introduced herself to him at an event to say how pleased she was to work with him and participate in the council. The general responded, "Yes, I see you are the only woman serving on the council." She responded, "Do you want to know what I think about that?" When the general replied, "Yes," she said, "I am also the only council member that can walk in the room wearing red pumps."

There were many rewarding moments for Joy during the time

she led the NCDBA. In 2009, she was part of a group of five that traveled to Afghanistan to visit the troops deployed there for Christmas. I commented to her how that took bravery, and she said, "One thing I have learned in my experience is to say yes! You can always get your name off the list, but if you say no, you never make the list." I think that is an excellent rule to live by.

Working with the military was the most rewarding part for Joy. She said, "The men and women who serve and defend our country undergo rigorous training, and the sacrifices they make are many. Everyone should have an opportunity to see that up close and personal."

Joy had learned her lesson about overstaying your welcome in an organization. She knew she had established a solid infrastructure and was confident it would thrive as an organization for many years. She knew it was time to pass the baton. After seven years in the role, she notified the board of directors she would be stepping down.

Desiring to have her own business and help other non-profits run the administrative part of the business, Joy started Business Resources Management (BRM) and added a woman-owned business and entrepreneur to her resume. Her first client was the Sanford Area Growth Alliance as the consulting CEO. This opportunity provided a good client base for BRM. Along with the Sanford, NC Chamber of Commerce and Economic Development, Joy created an organizational structure allowing the community to grow industry and create jobs while supporting small businesses. The accomplishments from this collaboration were many: Central Carolina Enterprise Park was developed, brand recognition for the community was improved to attract site selectors, opportunities for additional revenue streams were created, and a new visitors program was designed to attract visitors to the community.

Another client, Sanford Contractors, asked Joy to take a full-time position with the organization as the VP of Support Services. She accepted and soon found God's hand was at work in the timing. During the pandemic, the work of Sanford Contractors was considered essential, and she could stay employed. The role placed her in a position to interact with truck drivers and mechanics. She tapped back into her life as a wife and mother when her husband was a truck driver. She had lived their life and could respect their viewpoints. As a leader, it is essential to relate to someone on their level and tap into something important to them to earn their respect. Joy said, "It is important to realize everyone in the organization is needed and serves an important role in delivering the product or service."

Her position required her to handle the logistics for the company and manage the transfer of heavy equipment on job sites. This meant work boots, blue jeans, and a hard hat. Joy said, "It changed my whole identity, from red pumps and dresses to work boots and blue jeans. It was an identity crisis for who I was as a person." She continued to say, "One day, I was praying and asking God, 'How much longer do I need to be here?' I am drowning here." She laughed and said, "It was like I heard God say, 'Joy, stand up, you're in the kiddie pool.'"

Today, she has gotten out of the kiddie pool and continues to grow BRM, developing a client base that will benefit greatly from her expertise in accounting, human resources, and strategic planning.

Joy is also the president and founder of Children in His Care, an organization that helps families with funeral expenses when they lose a child under 18. She recently published her first children's book, *The Adventures of the Little Excavators*. The five excavators in the book are named for her five grandchildren.

Having experienced Joy's sound advice firsthand and knowing her strengths are building collaborative teams and creating an agenda to move a group of people together to a common goal for the greater good of the company and community, I asked her what she would say to the leaders reading this book.

Joy's List:

- Surround yourself with people smarter than you.

- Do not get distracted. Stay focused on the ultimate vision.

- No decision is still a decision, and it is a default decision. You need to be confident to decide and move forward.

- You never want to be the person who prevents members of the team from being able to do their job because you cannot reach a decision.

Knowing how important her faith is to her, I asked her to tell me about her faith and how that goes to work with her. She said, "Wherever I am put, God has me there for a reason, and it is about the people I can help, and I take that very seriously. When someone comes back and says I made a difference in their career or life, I know I've done my job."

"What would you tell your younger self?" I asked. She answered, "Don't be so overly driven that you do not have balance. And don't let the negative things people say about you define you as a person."

Finally, I asked her, "What's next?" She replied with determination, "I am more focused than I have ever been on my company. I want to continue growing Children in His Care to help families when they need it most. I have another book I want to write. Beyond that, I am not sure; God hasn't told me yet."

TAKEAWAYS

1. **Determination Overcomes Obstacles**: Joy's journey from being told she couldn't progress further in her banking career due to a lack of degree to earning her bachelor's degree with distinction, all while being a young mother and working, shows that obstacles can be overcome with determination and a clear vision.

2. **Self-awareness is Key**: Joy's realization that she preferred finance management for mid-size companies or small businesses rather than staying in an accounting firm underscores the importance of understanding oneself. Joy says, "Sometimes it is as important to know what you don't want as it is to know what you do want."

3. **Recognize the Value of Collaborative Partnerships**: The harmonious working relationship between Joy and Bill Martin at the Chamber of Commerce emphasizes the value of recognizing and cultivating beneficial partnerships. When two individuals complement each other's strengths, it can lead to mutual growth and success.

4. **Stand Your Ground in the Face of Adversity**: Despite facing a challenging work environment where her contributions and authority were undermined, Joy remained committed to her principles and the welfare of her team. Her experience highlights the challenges women often face in leadership positions and emphasizes the importance of recognizing one's worth, even in toxic environments.

5. **Resilience and Adaptability**: One of the most striking themes throughout Joy's life story is her remarkable ability to bounce back and adapt to new situations. From

being fired from the Chamber of Commerce to her marriage ending and having to start afresh in her professional life, she consistently showed resilience. This is further emphasized by her ability to transition from wearing "red pumps and dresses" to "work boots and blue jeans." This resilience teaches us the importance of adaptability in the face of change and adversity.

6. **The Value of Support and Community**: Another important lesson is the role of community and support. Whether it's the people who rallied around her after she got fired or the military personnel she interacted with, the importance of having a support system cannot be overstated. Her story reinforces the idea that even in the toughest of times, there are always people who will stand by you, and their support can be the difference between giving up and pushing forward.

7. **Skill Transfer and Continuous Learning**: Joy's transition from the Fayetteville Chamber of Commerce to founding the North Carolina Defense Business Association (NCDBA) highlights the value of transferable skills. Despite initially feeling she might not be qualified for the NCDBA role, she soon realized she could apply the skill set she had acquired at the Chamber. This emphasizes the importance of recognizing our value and the skills we possess and understanding that they can often be applied in various contexts.

8. **Guiding Principles for Leadership and Life**: Joy's insights, such as surrounding oneself with more intelligent people and staying focused on the vision, highlight key principles for effective leadership. Furthermore, her reflections on balance and not letting negativity define you offer profound advice on personal well-being and

self-worth. These points underscore the importance of self-awareness, decisive action, and maintaining a sense of purpose in leadership and life.

Joy's journey, with all its challenges and successes, is a testament to the power of perseverance, adaptability, and the importance of community and support. Her story can inspire readers to face adversities head-on, value the skills and experiences they possess, and continuously strive for personal and professional growth.

REFLECTIONS

"The only place success comes before work is in the dictionary."

Vince Lombardi

CHAPTER THIRTEEN

Building Your Personal Board of Directors

Navigating Career Growth

An African proverb says, "It takes a village to raise a child." It conveys the message that it takes many people – a village – to provide a safe, healthy environment for children, where they are provided with a safe space to develop and grow and realize their hopes and dreams.

The same could be said for corporate executives or aspiring entrepreneurs in the growth years of their career journey. It is important to realize you need a support team. John Donne, an English author from the seventeenth century, said, "No one is self-sufficient; everyone relies on others."

Everyone has an unofficial "personal board of directors." Translated, a close-knit group of people that you trust, and they have your best interest at heart. These people are the individuals you call first when facing a life event, career change, or significant challenge in your life. This group usually comprises family, close friends, and acquaintances. They may be teachers, colleagues, bosses, coaches, hairdressers, or therapists. Without a doubt, they will, in almost every situation, have had a high level of influence or impact on your life. Throughout your life, you have sought them out for advice, for comfort, to bounce something off them, ask for help, and on many different topics and circumstances. Sometimes, you followed the advice, and sometimes, you went in another direction, but if you reflect on those conversations, in almost every one, just having the conversation likely affected the outcome. I have found that sometimes, just talking it out helps me figure it out.

What if you intentionally set up a personal board of directors to provide your guidance? I highly recommend this if you have goals and aspirations to level up in your career, start a business, or reinvent yourself. It can be very impactful if you are stuck between options or know the next steps to take to make your goals a reality.

When you think about the people you would select to be on your board, I recommend you first think about what support you need, and this usually starts with identifying your learning opportunities and obstacles you may need to overcome. For example, let's say you are creative and dream of owning an art studio where you display and sell your work, but you are not good at the administrative side. You would need people on your board who could advise you on the legal and financial side of opening and operating a business.

In my current role, I travel quite often. One of the key members of my board is my husband, Lenny. When I decided an above-property role was my next career move, Lenny moved into the role of co-chair of my board. I am not saying that single women cannot accomplish what I have and more, but when you are married or have a significant other, it is crucial to have their buy-in and support to alleviate the stress in your career and your personal life. Without my co-chair, my life would look a lot different. As you think about what the next phase of your life looks like, don't forget to consider the people who will be affected by your success. Recognize that their life will change too, and collaborating with them will help avoid landmines that could potentially damage the relationship, be a deterrent to achieving your goals, or worse, cause you to quit because it is too hard to juggle both.

For those who do not currently have a significant other, have a good friend who can support you if you are in a position that requires long hours or travel. I love coming home to live plants and a pet. Someone doing the yard work or retrieving the packages from the front porch can alleviate stress and allow you to focus on the work. My husband is a God send; I come home to a full refrigerator, a happy and healthy dog, and thriving plants. This means I thrive because home is where the heart is, and the heart needs to be healthy and happy for everything else to fall into place.

Including family members on your board of directors is undoubtedly an option. However, family dynamics can be interesting, and without careful consideration of the health of the relationship, it could create chaos on your board and with the family. In most families, your close family, parents, and siblings want only the best for you, making them great candidates. However, sometimes, family members cannot step outside the family bond to provide the honesty you need from your board members. Often, your family has little to no idea about what you do when you go to work. The other family issue can be their fear you will fail because they love you and do not want to see you get hurt; they focus on the worst that can happen.

My board consists of two family members: my dad and my sister. Both have great minds for business, and I can always count on them to be honest with me if I ask for advice. I save my mother for those conversations when someone has dashed my dreams, and I can call her, and she will say, because she is my mama and she loves me, "Lovell, you can do anything you set your mind to."

I would also like to point out that having members on your board whom you aspire to emulate is also important. Is there someone you know who has already blazed the trail you are starting? If you want to be a CEO, find a CEO to add to your board. When I decided I wanted to run my first marathon, the first call I made was to someone that I knew had run many marathons. I asked her how I should get started, what advice she would give me, and which marathon I should run first. That 20-minute phone call gave me the confidence to put my foot out the door for that first training run, and before I knew it, I was running two marathons a year for the next six years.

You may also have people who already provide professional services for you, like your accountant or financial planner. When I started my company, I had my lawyer, accountant, and financial advisor on my board. We would schedule planning calls to discuss tasks related to creating the LLC, banking, and legal requirements.

Some additional considerations for your board: take the Goldilocks approach: don't make it too big or too small; make it just right. If it is too small, you may not have all the areas of expertise you will need. If it is too big, there may be too many differences of opinion, and that will add to your confusion and make decision-making even harder. You should also make sure it is diverse. Too many like-minded people may squash out-of-the-box thinking. A dynamic group of people from different industries, cultures, and backgrounds can become the cast of influencers and mentors that help you achieve the future you aspire to. Most of all, select people you trust, and you know without any doubt they have your best interest at heart.

As you have been reading this chapter, you have probably already started thinking about the people in your life who are unofficially on your board today. Before you enlist members for your intentional board of directors, you will need to complete some prework. First, put your goals in writing. You may already be very clear about your future, but writing your vision down will authenticate your plan. The next step will be to identify the steps to get there. During this process, you will see where you have limited knowledge of navigating certain areas. This is where you will need help. One of the mistakes people make that keeps them from being successful is not admitting what they do not know. Own those learning moments so that you will be sure to include people who can teach you and guide you through those areas of opportunity. Now that you have organized the vision and process, you can determine who will best serve you in this endeavor.

Do not select people just because you don't want to hurt their feelings, because they are your closest friend, or because you have one of your siblings on the board, so you should include them all. Remember, you must be intentional about the people who serve on your board; they must be someone who will support you, align with your values, bring expertise to the process, and understand the vision. Be intentional about your choices. After all, this is not a popularity contest; this is your future.

Now that you have determined who you would like to be on your personal board of directors, you must lay out a plan for making it official. The first step is to develop your "why" speech. Why do you feel the need to bring together this group of people at this time in your career? It is likely driven by the career goals that you have. Is it an imminent opportunity or a personal strategic growth plan for your long-term career? You will need to clearly articulate why you need to create a board, your vision for how individuals will support you, and how you envision interacting with them.

A word of caution: prepare yourself for the possibility of someone you have selected saying they do not have the time to serve. The opportunity for this to happen is rare, but in some cases, the individuals you choose may be in a position that does not allow them the bandwidth to take on more. In this case, they are likely trying to be fair to you by saying they do not want to fail in such an important task. Don't take it personally.

Once you have confirmed the people who will serve, you must respect the communication cadence. In some cases, you will connect with individuals one on one. For individuals who provide professional services, you may have meetings to collaborate with multiple attendees at one time. In all communication, be respectful of the individual's time. Schedule calls and meetings in advance, be punctual, and have an agenda to ensure the meeting is efficient. Treat your personal board like a real board of directors.

Remember, in the case of a personal board of directors, you will likely need to act on the decisions or advice presented in the discussions. Always provide follow-up to the individuals who participated in giving you guidance or advice. Share your successes.

Consider it an honor if you are ever asked to serve on someone's board. They are saying they trust you and believe you can help them become the next best version of themselves. That said, it is a huge responsibility, and you must be committed to investing the time and accepting the responsibility of always being 100% honest. Most importantly, you must balance your judgment and curiosity in every conversation. Not everyone gets to the same place in the same way. We may leave Washington, DC, for Philadelphia simultaneously, except you may take an Acela, and I may choose to drive. The point is we will still arrive at the same place, but the journey may be different.

Whatever journey you choose, enjoy!

TAKEAWAYS

1. **Importance of a Support System**: Just as the African adage suggests raising a child is a collective effort, this chapter reinforces the idea that the people around us nurture our personal and professional growth. It emphasizes that we're not isolated in our journey; our decisions and paths are influenced by trusted individuals who provide guidance, perspective, and support.

2. **Intentional Composition of a Personal Board of Directors**: One shouldn't haphazardly or passively rely on their existing network. Instead, there's value in intentionally identifying and assembling a board that fills one's knowledge and skill gaps. This board can comprise a mix of personal and professional contacts, but each should serve a distinct purpose in offering expertise, providing emotional support, or challenging one's views.

3. **The Value of Diverse Perspectives**: It's tempting to surround oneself with like-minded individuals, but the chapter underscores the importance of seeking out those with diverse viewpoints. This provides a fuller understanding of situations and can challenge and enrich one's personal beliefs and convictions. A robust board offers a mix of affirmation and constructive criticism.

4. **Navigating Familial Relationships**: While family can be an immense source of support, their involvement in one's personal board of directors should be approached with discernment. The chapter brings out the dual edge of familial ties: the genuine concern and emotional support they bring, coupled with the potential for biases and overprotection. It's essential to differentiate between objective business advice and emotional comfort, under-

standing the different roles family members can play.

5. **Emulate Your Aspirations**: Seek out individuals who represent who you want to become. If your goal is to attain a particular position, role, or accomplishment, having someone on your board who has already achieved that is invaluable. Their experience, insights, and advice are directly pertinent and can expedite your journey. As illustrated, aiming to complete a marathon is far more achievable with guidance from a seasoned marathoner.

6. **Strive for Balance and Diversity**: A well-composed board is neither too small nor too large. A small board may lack the breadth of expertise you need, while a larger one might result in information overload or conflicting guidance. Moreover, diversity in your board – spanning industries, backgrounds, and experiences – is paramount to fostering innovative thinking and offering varied perspectives, leading to well-rounded decisions.

7. **Purposeful Selection and Induction**: Forming your board should be intentional based on merit and alignment with your objectives. It's critical to avoid including members out of mere sentimentality or obligation. Before formalizing their roles, ensure you're clear about your aspirations and articulate your expectations from each member, providing a compelling rationale for their inclusion. This ensures both parties are on the same page regarding commitment and contribution.

8. **Accountability and Professionalism**: Your interactions with your personal board of directors should be conducted with the utmost professionalism. Valuing their time, coming prepared, and being organized are essential. However, while the board provides direction

and advice, the responsibility for action and implementation remains yours. Keeping them informed about your progress and being accountable for the advice enhances the relationship's efficacy.

These lessons highlight the multi-faceted nature of support systems, provide a roadmap for anyone looking to establish or refine their own board, and underscore the significance of a strategic approach to building one. The right board can serve as a powerful catalyst for personal and professional growth, but its composition, management, and utilization require careful consideration and diligence.

REFLECTIONS

"Success comes when people act together; failure tends to happen alone."

Deepak Chopra

Chapter Fourteen

A Journey of Transformation and Reinvention

Reverend Dr. Martha Scott

Martha's life journey is a testament to the power of transformation. If you have ever wondered if you can transition from one industry to another or completely reinvent yourself in the same company or industry, I believe Martha's story will have you saying, "Yes, I can!"

Entering the workforce at 16 years old, Martha's determination was evident from the beginning. Her college years took her to the University of Tennessee Chattanooga, where she earned a bachelor's degree in finance in 1998.

Finance wasn't truly where Martha envisioned forging her career path. She said her decision was based on the hypothesis that no matter how much money she earned, she would know how to manage it. Even in her early twenties, strong traits of independence were showing up. Martha's first job out of college was industrial collections for a large gas firm. The company had multiple locations within the United States. At twenty-three, Martha explored an opportunity to make a lateral move with the gas company and move to New Jersey. You can imagine how Martha's family felt about her leaving Tennessee and moving to the Northeast. That did not deter her. She was looking for a way out of Small Town USA. New Jersey wasn't a choice — it could have been anywhere; she just needed to spread her wings and fly.

In addition to a strong trait of independence, Martha has always craved a challenge, and in the absence of a challenge, she becomes bored quickly. A year later, she was looking for a better fit in Knoxville, Tennessee, and took a new position in the accounting department at a small engineering firm in Oak Ridge. Desiring to continue to grow her career and finances, she moved a year later to TeamHealth, a prominent physician practice management company in Knoxville. After about a year in her accounting job, she began to realize that finance did not stimulate her enough and that even though that was where her degree was, she needed to move on.

Next came Martha's first successful reinvention, and it started with a trip to the human resources department to inquire if there were other jobs within the company for which she could be considered. She only had one caveat: it needed to be anything but accounting. Fortunately, the company's vice president of marketing learned of Martha's inquiry and interviewed her for a marketing specialist role. The VP of marketing was impressed that Martha had proactively sought another position and decided to give her a chance, even though she had no marketing training or experience. It was an entry-level position, but Martha quickly learned the task assigned to her. The VP of marketing recognized that Martha needed to be challenged, and not long into her first role in marketing, she was promoted to her second position as a proposal writer.

Coming to the end of her twenties, Martha's love for education led her to go back to school and pursue an MBA. Working for a company with highly educated physicians, she assumed she might need a higher degree to continue her growth in the company. Besides, Martha said, "I love education; it is what I do for fun." We should add determination to Martha's trait because, at the age of 30, she successfully graduated with an MBA.

The next move for Martha was with a small training company, a woman-owned business, where she became the marketing director. Three years into the role, the company was a casualty of the

2008 financial crash, and she was downsized. The timing could not have seemed worse because, at the time, she was a single mom of a two-year-old.

It was also about this time that Martha felt called to ministry. Even though she heard a calling to help people and do something purposefully, she argued with God, saying, "This is a bad idea; I am not cut out for this." God had a different plan and had already placed her in the sight of her pastor and spiritual mentor. After prayer and consideration, Martha decided to go back to school and pursue a Master of Divinity. It took more than six years to complete, and all the while, she was back at TeamHealth, working a full-time job and raising her daughter as a single mother. Wow! During the interview, Martha and I chuckled at how tired we felt to think about the schedule she kept for almost seven years. That said, in the summer of 2008, she began seminary.

So, if you have lost track of the pivots in Martha's professional journey, let's recap. She spent just under five years in finance, moved to marketing, had a successful career in marketing for 15 years, and, during that time, she received an MBA and a Master of Divinity. I guess you CAN do anything you set your mind to.

While Martha was in seminary, she got married. Now that she had a two-income home, she was able to work part-time while she finished seminary. In 2014, at forty years old, Martha Scott was ordained an elder in the United Methodist Church. Martha's first assignment was to be the administrative pastor of a church with a congregation of 600 people. As she began her role, the church's beloved pastor of 22 years fell ill and had to step down. In his place, a new young pastor was assigned who soon thereafter experienced moral failure, significantly and negatively impacting the congregation. As a result, just a short time into this new chapter in her life, Martha was called on to become the leader and healer of this broken church community. While working to lead the church through that difficult time, she was dealing with a loss of her own. Her marriage of five years ended in divorce.

Her second assignment was as senior pastor for a smaller church with a congregation of 250. Martha's favorite part of her job was preaching. She loved to preach. She was thriving and making a difference in the lives of her parishioners. She was living out her purpose. Soon, the challenges she experienced in the church she moved from would seem like a walk in the park when she fulfilled her commitment to her calling during a worldwide pandemic.

In March 2020, when the world shut down, Martha had to navigate all the responsibilities of a pastor in a new and different way. With all her education, no degree prepared her for what was ahead. During COVID-19, everyone found themselves making decisions they never had to make before. There was so much unknown, and many decisions had to be made based on what you knew on that day, in the moment. There was little clarity, and any decision made would not please 100% of the people.

Unless you have been a pastor or part of a pastor's close family, you do not realize the actual weight of the responsibility. A pastor takes on the pain and the emotions of their congregation, and during 2020 and 2021, there was an immense amount of loss, pain, and overwhelming emotions in just about everyone's lives. While navigating virtually and still trying to serve her church with funerals and weddings, Martha also dealt with loss. Four people very close to her died during the pandemic. She had a 13-year-old daughter that she needed to ensure survived her own disappointments and trials of the pandemic.

Martha began to wrestle with one of the most significant decisions she would make. For two years, she prayed about leaving her duties as pastor. Finally realizing she needed to practice self-care and be fully present with her daughter, she made the heart-wrenching decision to step back from her pastoral duties. Her church understood how hard this decision was for her and surrounded her with love and support.

Today, Martha is back at TeamHealth as a project manager. She has found a balance in her life and is enjoying the last two years with her daughter at home before she goes to college.

At the conclusion of my interview with Martha, we discussed that all her direct supervisors have been women throughout her corporate career. I asked her to elaborate on traits she saw in those female leaders. She emphasized the profound impact of a female leader, praising their emotional intelligence, strategic thinking, and excellent intuition.

When I asked Martha what was next, she said, "I am going to have dinner with my daughter, get up in the morning, have a cup of coffee, go to work, and maybe take a yoga class." I applaud Martha for recognizing when it is time to take a break, practice physical and emotional self-care, and prioritize her most important role as a mother. She embodies the spirit of reinvention, and while she's content now, her journey is far from over. Her story serves as a beacon of hope and inspiration for all; I am certain we have not yet seen the last phase of the career and life of Reverend Doctor Martha Scott.

TAKEAWAYS

1. **Embrace Change and Reinvention**: Martha's journey from finance to marketing, then to ministry, and back to a corporate role showcases the power of adaptability. It's never too late to reinvent oneself or to pivot in a new direction.

2. **Prioritize Self-Care**: Despite her deep commitment to her work and her community, Martha recognized when she needed to step back for the sake of her mental and emotional health. Prioritizing self-care is not only essential for personal well-being but also for the quality of our work and the impact we can have on others.

3. **Listen to Inner Guidance**: Whether it's a calling to ministry or a realization that a particular path isn't fulfilling, listening to one's inner voice and intuition is crucial. Martha's story underscores the importance of aligning with personal purpose and values.

4. **Value Education**: Martha's love for education, not just as a means to an end but as a passion, is evident in her pursuits of an MBA, Master of Divinity, and Doctor of Ministry. Continuous learning is both personally enriching and professionally advantageous.

5. **Be Resilient in the Face of Adversity**: Whether dealing with professional challenges, personal losses, or global crises like the pandemic, Martha's resilience shines through. The ability to navigate hardships with grace and determination is a testament to her strength.

6. **Value and Nurture Relationships**: Throughout her journey, the importance of relationships, whether with

mentors, family, or her congregation, is evident. Human connections provide support, open doors, and create a sense of belonging.

7. **Leadership Traits Matter**: Martha's observation about the leadership qualities she admired in her female supervisors — emotional intelligence, strategic thinking, and intuition — underscores the importance of these traits in today's complex and interconnected world.

8. **Stay Present in the Moment**: Martha's response to what's next — focusing on the immediate moments with her daughter, work, and self-care — emphasizes the importance of being present. While it's essential to have long-term goals, finding joy and purpose in daily life is equally crucial.

Martha's story serves as a testament to the multifaceted journeys life can offer and the many ways one can find purpose, connection, and fulfillment.

<u>REFLECTIONS</u>

"She believed she could, so she did."

R.S. Grey

CHAPTER FIFTEEN

Mentors, Protectors, and Teachers

The Impactful Men in My Journey

I would be remiss if I did not dedicate a chapter in this book to the men in my life who have helped me become the woman and leader I am today. In life and business, I have been blessed to have wonderful role models who mentored and invested in me. I learned to be a leader through their example, encouragement, and correction.

My paternal granddaddy, Rev. Andrew B. Whittington, was a pastor. His work in ministry spanned more than 50 years. Some of my earliest memories as a child were attending his church and spending time at my grandparents' house. On Saturday mornings, my granddaddy would go to his office at the church and work on his sermon for Sunday morning. He would often take me with him, and as he was writing his sermon, he would discuss it with me. My heart is full as I think of the seeds planted in my soul during those sessions. Granddaddy even had a sermon on leadership. The theme of the message was *to be a good leader, one must be a good follower*. I often say that my granddaddy could find a reason to have people in his church every night of the week. His journey as a pastor often involved going into a church that needed help. He had a way of going into a church that was divided and had been losing members, and successfully growing the congregation to record levels.

In my career, similar to Granddaddy's assignments to underperforming churches, I have often been assigned to underperforming hotels. I liken my approach to improving these hotels to the same principles my granddaddy applied in church. First, he identified members who had a desire to improve the situation and were open to change, and he rallied those people to be part of the solution. It is true that there is strength in numbers. He set up structure and policy and set an example of following the rules he asked of others. For me, Granddaddy was one of the first of many examples of leadership by example. His example of following Christ caused his parishioners to want to follow him, allowing him to reestablish the church.

Years later, I had the opportunity to work in my dad's office. My Uncle Ray was my direct supervisor. Uncle Ray also leads by example; he would never ask you to perform a task he was unwilling to do himself. I also learned gratitude from Uncle Ray. At the end of every workday, he would stand by the door and thank team members for a good day's work as they would leave to go home. The culture that my uncle created was one of the first experiences I had of a true work family. He took time to know his associates and not only know them but know the names of their spouses and children.

One of my favorite quotes is, "The speed of the pack is determined by the leader." The lead dog in the pack always sets the pace. As a leader, you must show up and perform at a level that is setting the pace for your team. That model is required of you not only in the output of the work but also in your values.

My daddy, Rev. Jim Whittington, is a television evangelist. He started preaching one year before I was born. To say my dad has significantly influenced my life would be an understatement. I have always been a daddy's girl. From the time I could walk, he would bring me up to stand next to him while he was preaching. I am certain my confidence on stage comes from those early years in church when my daddy and granddaddy put me on the platform. I have often said my dad was the push behind my drive, and I have a lot of drive. The top three things I learned from my dad that I use as a corporate leader are: practice makes perfect, always follow up, and your word is your bond. These leadership lessons were not just learned from a father's guidance while bringing up a daughter, but from years of working for him and alongside him in the ministry.

When I began to sing, Daddy would tell me, "You need to sing a song at least 100 times before you sing it in public." He would also say, "Stand flat-footed and hit the last note perfectly, because the last note is what people will remember you by. You can sing the whole song perfectly, but if you fail in the end, that is what they remember." I would say that stands true in being a corporate executive; you must hold out like you started and finish strong in every project, meeting, and professional relationship. Inconsistency can be a career killer, but a strong finish can make an impact.

Daddy was always – and still is – a stickler for follow-up. If he asked me to handle something that required someone to call me back or get me information, I learned very young in my adult life that saying they had not called me back was not an acceptable answer. I have spent my hospitality career in the commercial strategy discipline. Not being shy about following up or chasing the deal has undoubtedly contributed to my success as a salesperson. Additionally, when I became responsible for a large team, the department's success depended on my thoughtful and organized approach to following up on multiple tasks, hotels, and direct reports. It really is the secret to my sauce as to how I can manage a career and two houses and still have a quality of life with my family and friends.

Finally, Daddy always taught his children that if you tell someone you will do something, do it. Your word is your bond. I am not even sure that needs any further explanation. That is not only how we should approach our work lives but how we should live our whole lives.

When I was 10, my mother married my stepfather, James R. Hales. His friends and family called him Robert. He was a veteran and served in the Vietnam War. He was a second father to Joy and me for 32 years. We suddenly lost him to a heart attack when he was 60.

Earlier in his life, when Robert left to go to war, he had a wife and daughter; however, when he came home, his wife had divorced him and moved to another state with his daughter. To my knowledge, he never saw his daughter again. Robert was in printing, and when he married Mom, he was a typesetter for a printing shop. His work as a typesetter exposed him to a great amount of information across many topics, and he was a brilliant man.

The biggest life lesson Robert taught me was during my teenage years. I was going through a very rebellious time, and often, Robert would sit me down and try to talk some sense into me. I remember he would always say, "I don't want you to learn the hard way like I did, learn from my mistakes." Indeed, we can often learn what to do from people, but there is also an equal opportunity to learn what *not* to do.

I did not heed Robert's advice at the time, although my journey could have been easier if I had. What I know now is that every mistake should be a learning moment, and as a leader, it is important that you empower your team to make decisions, recognizing they will not always make sound decisions and they will make mistakes. As their mentor, it is your job to help them learn and grow from those mistakes. Encourage them to work backward from the outcome and evaluate what could have been done differently to avoid failures the next time. The worst decision is no decision; your success depends on those around you being confident to make decisions in their area of responsibility or in your absence.

Robert would call Joy and me "Kid." It was a term of endearment. Recently, my sister shared with me that she had worked for a man who would occasionally call her "Kid." She was not offended by it and felt the relationship was such that he viewed her as someone he wanted to take under his wing and help grow. Often, we get too hung up on someone using nicknames or something other than our name to address us. Instead of considering it may be demeaning or a put-down, perhaps you should ask yourself if that person just feels comfortable with you and wants to support you and your growth. If it is not inappropriate or makes you uncomfortable, it is probably okay.

In 1988, Lenny Casiero entered my life. We were the poster couple for love at first sight and opposites attract. Lenny and I have been married for 35 years, and I would like to think we have positively impacted each other. To tell you how Lenny influenced my leadership style, I need to go back to my teenage years when I lived with another Scorpio, my sister Joy. My sister was the good daughter, and I was not. She kept a spotless room; mine was that of a typical teenager with no organization, which created constant frustration for my mother. Fact: Joy would not allow me in her room for fear I would mess it up. Scorpios are apparently very organized, and in 1988, I married one. I was a bit more organized and had learned some good housekeeping practices by then, but I was still far from meeting the organizational skills of my new husband. For the first year we were married, he would patiently collect all my personal belongings I left around the house and place them in a neat pile in the area I used as a dressing room. I have often said Lenny was the daughter his mother never had. His organizational skills, at home and in his job as a mixologist, have always been top-notch. The clothes come out of the dryer one minute before it stops. We have a backup for all our food staples, and when you use the backup, you put the needed item on the list. According to Lenny, that is how you never run out of anything.

I do believe that opposites attract but that you begin to complement each other over the years of marriage. During the last 35 years, Lenny has certainly complemented my ability to be a better organizer. I am confident it has impacted my ability to be well-traveled, manage multiple tasks as a leader, and organize a plethora of projects across the teams I have led. It is my opinion that good time management starts with a life list.

Lenny also taught me the value of trust in a relationship. Our professions could have wreaked havoc on our relationship – I worked days, and he worked nights. We had an understanding when he was bartending and I was a bar patron. If either of us started getting hit on, I would leave and meet him at our favorite spot after he got off work. After 20 years of marriage, we would often get asked the question, "What is your secret to success?" and without hesitation, we would always say that we trust each other as much as we love each other. In 2005, when I started my multi-property role, I was traveling 80% of the time, and that travel consisted of meetings during the day and dinners at night. Our trust never waned; it prevailed and helped us get through those times apart.

Lastly, Lenny has supported me with unwavering dedication. He believes in me and encourages me to achieve my goals and dreams. I am blessed to have found this in a husband. I never take for granted that behind every successful woman, there is a very good man.

Because I grew up in ministry, I was always surrounded by preachers. Two preachers I consider spiritual fathers and mentors are Rev. Dr. Roscoe Connor, pastor of Faith Tabernacle in Asheville, NC, and Bishop Herro Blair, Faith Cathedral Deliverance Centre in Kingston, Jamaica.

I do not remember Rev. Connor not being in my life because he was already a family friend when I was born. He watched me grow up. When I ran the television ministry, he could not have been more supportive; he encouraged me on days I did not see a way through. He would invite me to his church to minister in song and message. There were two things I learned from Roscoe that I will never forget. He taught me your words are the first and most powerful touch you leave on someone. The power of life and death is in the tongue. Then he would say, "But when you leave someone, always leave a physical touch on them – a pat on the arm or back, a hug, a handshake, a kiss; your spirit passes through them when you touch them."

I will never forget my favorite sermon Roscoe preached. One must toil in the valley to enjoy the view from the mountaintop. If you do not do the work in the valley, there will be no view when you reach the top. That is so true in the corporate world. You must realize that belonging at the executive level should not come from your gender or ethnicity, but from the quality of work you do on the way up.

Bishop Herro Blair is one of the most successful entrepreneurs I know. His story of where he came from to where he is today is truly amazing. I was in my thirties when I remember meeting Bishop Blair for the first time.

The missionary division of the Christian Correspondence Church was Caribbean Missions. Dr. Carl Hughes originally started the organization and introduced me to ministry and mission work in the Caribbean. When Dr. Hughes passed, he bequeathed the organization to me. I was honored to continue the work. We worked in many of the Caribbean islands, but when Dad returned to the ministry, we focused on Jamaica. Without the guidance of Bishop Blair, I am sure our work would have met more challenges. Bishop taught me that protocol matters. He consistently executed protocol and demanded it from the people who worked for him and with him. You knew when you participated in a church service at one of Bishop's churches, you were under the rule of the service's protocol.

Many organizations, especially startups, fail because their protocols are too lax. Meetings should start on time, and minutes should be recorded. Billing and financials should have calendared due dates and be adhered to. Standard operating procedures should guide people. All these things and more are the protocol of running a business.

I also learned from Bishop how to conduct business in a different culture. I could not go into Jamaica and expect to communicate and conduct business as I did in the United States. I would have failed. I learned that I had to adapt to the culture I was working in, which meant adjusting my expectations of others, my communication, and my leadership skills, all while conducting the business I was there to do. I must have learned and adapted well because we expanded our television ministry into Jamaica, raised millions of dollars to support projects on the island, and, in 1997, organized an island-wide crusade where more than 20,000 people attended the services.

Suppose you do business in different countries or even other states within the United States. In that case, I highly recommend you understand how the culture drives how people work and conduct business. You may succeed without doing so, but I promise the road will be a little more challenging, and the trip will take longer. It is also important to understand the culture of the people you lead. You cannot lead someone if you do not understand their belief system and where they came from because all that matters when trying to motivate them.

In my professional life, I have had the opportunity to work with some very accomplished and intelligent people. These leaders exhibited the values I learned from my family and spiritual mentors. I will not call out the companies or name the individuals. I think some will know who they are should they read this book.

I am grateful for the men who gave me my first opportunity, believed in me, and saw something I did not even see in myself. Some gave me exposure to key decision-makers along the way to support my career growth. I appreciate them trusting me to serve on boards and allowing me to truly be a voice at the table. The times when they challenged or corrected me have only made me stronger. When my career led me in a new direction, I appreciated the ones who continued to take my call. I especially take my hat off to the ones who showed they truly wanted what was best for me, not the company. To the ones who did not take my first answer but forced me to be curious, thank you. To the ones who saw value in me and helped me learn how to execute from that value, you own some of the credit for where I am today.

I also want to thank the men who were condescending to me – you taught me to fight. For the ones who looked at me and saw a sex object, you taught me how powerful that could be when used correctly. For the ones who just showed up acting like a bully every day, you taught me what insecurity left untreated can do to someone. For the ones who were mean to me, you taught me to be kind. For the ones who never gave me credit for helping to grow the business, you taught me to recognize those who contribute to my success.

Look around! The people in your life, whether men or women, family or colleagues, contribute to or tear down your ability to succeed at every encounter. It is up to you what you take away from those interactions. They may last a mere moment, a decade, or a lifetime, but you can determine how they define you.

TAKEAWAYS

1. **Leadership Through Personal Example**: Both my grandfather and Uncle Ray demonstrated the essence of leading by example. For Granddaddy, it was by personally adhering to the same rules he set for others, showcasing a commitment to the path of Christ. For Uncle Ray, it was never delegating a task he wouldn't do himself and emphasizing the importance of gratitude.

2. **Unity and Collaboration**: Granddaddy knew the importance of harnessing the power of unity. By identifying individuals who shared a common vision, he was able to build a cohesive force to drive positive change. He recognized that a collaborative effort is often stronger and more effective than isolated endeavors.

3. **Consistency and Commitment**: My dad emphasized the value of practicing diligently, finishing strong, and the significance of the final impression. Consistency in actions and commitments is vital in leadership. In the same vein, the saying "The speed of the pack is determined by the leader" accentuates that a leader's performance, values, and principles become the standard for the team.

4. **The Importance of Follow-Up and Integrity**: My dad also underscored the necessity of diligent follow-ups and the idea that one's word should be sacrosanct. If you commit to something, it's paramount to see it through, and failing to follow up or not keeping one's promises erodes trust and credibility.

5. **Learning from Mistakes**: From Robert's life, we learn about the importance of gaining wisdom from our experiences. Instead of enduring hardships or repeating mis-

takes, paying attention to the advice and lessons from those who've been there before is vital. This not only applies to personal life but is a principle that can be carried over to leadership and team management. The essence of this lesson is to view mistakes as opportunities to learn and grow.

6. **The Value of Trust and Support in Relationships**: Through the story of my relationship with Lenny, the immense significance of trust is highlighted. Whether it's in personal relationships or the workplace, trust is a foundational element. When trust exists, challenges are more manageable, and partners or team members feel empowered and supported. Furthermore, being surrounded by supportive individuals can significantly bolster one's confidence and determination to pursue goals and dreams.

7. **The Power of Words and Touch**: Rev. Dr. Roscoe Connor emphasized two vital points: the impact of words and the significance of physical touch. Words can uplift or destroy, and it's paramount to be mindful of what we say. Physical touch, on the other hand, can create deep connections and leave lasting impressions, reinforcing the human need for connection and intimacy. In leadership, these lessons underscore the importance of effective communication and building meaningful relationships.

8. **The Importance of Protocols and Cultural Understanding**: As presented through Bishop Blair's teachings, upholding protocols ensures consistency and effectiveness in operations, which is vital for business success. Moreover, understanding and respecting the local cultural nuances is essential when conducting business or operations across cultures. Leaders who demonstrate cultural awareness and flexibility tend to forge stronger relation-

ships and achieve greater success in diverse environments.

Each of these lessons showcases the profound impact that family and mentors can have on an individual's leadership journey, providing timeless principles that are applicable across various domains.

<u>REFLECTIONS</u>

"Faith is taking the first step even when you don't see the whole staircase."

Martin Luther King Jr.

Chapter Sixteen

The Attributes of Female Leaders

I n 2019, I attended the *Elevate* program offered by the Castell Project. The organization specifically focuses on helping women find more leadership presence in the hotel industry and industries that provide services in the field of hospitality. It was a wonderful experience that came with four personal coaching sessions. Until this opportunity, I never really thought about the statistics around men versus women in hospitality. I learned that at the management level, it is almost a 50/50 split between women and men. In some cases, depending on the company presenting the statistics, there are about 7% more women in management than men. The pendulum swings significantly as you continue to track the statistics through director, VP, SVP, and finally, a C-suite position. In 2022, the Castell Project reported that at the C-suite level, women represented a ratio of only 1 to 10.

I have worked for and with some amazing male and female leaders. I agree there can be significant differences in their style and approach to leadership, but I also think there are many similarities. Speaking from my own experience, the common attributes of people I consider exceptional leaders are being highly energetic, being tenured in their industry, and having worked their way up through the ranks, sometimes starting at an entry-level position. In most cases, they recognized the value of fueling their energy with a healthy lifestyle, including exercise, a good diet, and self-care practices. I benefitted from their motivational skills and trusted their authenticity. This book would not be complete without pointing out the differences in male and female attributes and why we need both applications.

As you read through these attributes, I encourage you to think about your own attributes as a leader. I am confident you will find opportunities to learn from both the female and male traits noted through my research. After compiling this list, I scored myself on each one from both lists. I completed a self-diagnostic of each attribute, rating my strength in that area on a scale of 1-5, with five being the strongest and one the weakest. It was a simple exercise, but seeing where I could improve or dial it back a little was eye-opening. The most significant learning moment for me was when I learned that some male attributes were my strongest and some female attributes ranked the lowest overall.

Each attribute is important; while some may be more feminine, they are all important. An attribute is a quality or feature regarded as a characteristic or inherent part of someone. Therefore, they enhance the circumstances in which they are applied.

Female Leadership Attributes:

1. **Emotional Intelligence**: Women tend to be more in tune with the feelings and needs of their team members, which can contribute to an ability to be more successful at transforming attitudes and beliefs. In many circumstances, women are more likely to bring a win-win approach to a negotiation. In this type of negotiation, the opposition rarely feels they lost.

2. **Humility and Self-Awareness**: Female leaders come with a more authentic approach to leadership, exhibiting less ego. They have a high level of respect for other people's perspectives and what they can contribute to the team and organization. When receiving feedback, women project a positive attitude. Practicing self-awareness al-

lows for a more accurate knowledge of their personal strengths and weaknesses. The opportunities identified are addressed by setting goals to improve.

3. **Empathy**: Women with an empathetic nature lead with kindness, approaching leadership as a service to others. Mentoring team members is vital, and striving for a nurturing and supportive work environment is very important. This empathetic quality can also lead to better conflict resolution and a culture founded on teamwork.

4. **Collaboration**: Female leaders are frequently seen as collaborative and inclusive. They tend to value and promote a team-oriented approach, emphasizing the importance of working together and fostering a sense of community within their organizations. Their teams often have a family-like feel. Elevating others is top of mind for most women in leadership. They approach relationships as strategic and transactional, fostering creative and innovative ideas.

5. **Adaptability**: Women in their domestic roles tend to be stronger when it comes to multitasking, which transfers to their leadership role. Female leaders are known for their adaptability and flexibility. They tend to be open to change, new ideas, and innovative solutions. A female leader's willingness to take on multiple roles within an organization can help them expand their responsibility and move up within the organization.

6. **Communication**: Mindful communication is often a strong suit of female leaders. They are skilled at active listening. Their communication style tends to be more open, approachable, and conducive to higher authenticity.

7. **Mentorship and Coaching**: Female leaders often excel in mentorship and coaching roles. They are more likely to invest time in developing the skills and careers of their team members, fostering a supportive and growth-oriented atmosphere. Women tend to provide more recognition and credit to the team and individual contribution to the organization's overall success. When it is necessary to provide constructive feedback, they are clear and concise.

8. **Resilience**: Women are very good at overcoming stress and adversity. Their resilience is often fueled by optimism. Female leaders often view failure as a form of helpful feedback. They are known for leading with enthusiasm and passion. They can take command of a situation and start moving towards a solution quickly when needed.

Male Leadership Attributes:

1. **Confidence**: Male leaders often project confidence, which can be perceived as a strong, decisive leadership style. This can be advantageous in situations where bold decision-making is required. It is not always the strongest attribute for women. They often see themselves as not ready for a promotion. Men are more likely to step out of their comfort zone, not second-guessing their ability to take on a promotion.

2. **Assertiveness**: Men are more impulsive and often take a "just do it approach" when giving directions. Conversely, women will direct from a "do it if you can get it right approach."

3. **Risk-Taking**: Men in leadership may be more inclined to take a calculated gamble. They often are willing to step

outside the box of conventional thinking, which can lead to innovative solutions and growth opportunities.

4. **Strategic Thinking**: Male leaders are often associated with strategic thinking and long-term planning. They are more likely to take a big-picture approach, focusing on setting organizational goals and creating a clear vision for the future.

5. **Inquisitive**: Men tend to be more inquisitive. They tend to gravitate towards data and metrics when making decisions and planning. They are drawn more towards the STEM methodology.

6. **Independence**: Many male leaders are seen as independent and self-reliant. They may be comfortable making autonomous decisions and taking ownership of their leadership responsibilities. This can cause them to be perceived as less communicative with the team.

7. **Assertive Negotiation**: In negotiation scenarios, male leaders are often viewed as assertive and competitive, which can be advantageous in certain business contexts. They are more inclined to negotiate from a position of strength and assert their interests.

8. **Vision**: As leaders, the confidence and approach to risk-taking often result in men being great visionaries. A strong leader should have a clear and inspiring vision for the future, and they should be able to communicate this vision to their team.

As corporations continue to evolve and ensure their culture has a strategy of achieving equity and inclusion for all genders and ethnic backgrounds, it will be important they acknowledge that leadership attributes are not determined by gender and avoid conforming to preconceived notions of gender roles. Leadership is about influence, vision, and the ability to bring about positive change, regardless of whether the leader is a woman or a man.

Everyone needs to take a giant step forward in dismantling stereotypes and fostering environments where people are valued for contributing to the overall good of a society built on inclusion and respect for others.

It is important to recognize that none of these attributes are exclusive to one gender. Leaders can possess a combination of these qualities, and the best leaders draw from a diverse set of attributes depending on the situation. Leaders are conditioned by where they came from, and there is a wide range of backgrounds and experiences among successful leaders. People are unique, and their leadership styles can also be very unique. The key to effective leadership is not in adhering to gender stereotypes but in understanding and embracing the diversity of leadership attributes.

As you navigate your career, be mindful not to put too much emphasis on seeking out teachers and mentors based on their gender or age, but on what they have accomplished, and their level of expertise in their scope of responsibility because that is what you can learn from them. Understanding if their leadership style will provide a culture where you can thrive is also important.

When honing your leadership skills, remember that to be a leader, you must lead in a way people will want to follow. The absolute one thing a leader must have is someone who will follow them. If you are not motivating and inspiring the people you lead, they will likely find someone else to follow.

In conclusion, effective leadership is about possessing a combination of these attributes, regardless of gender. It's also important to note that different leadership situations may require other qualities to be emphasized. It is crucial to strive for balance in these qualities and pause to determine which one will be most effective for the matter at hand.

TAKEAWAYS

1. **Diversity of Leadership Styles is Crucial**: One of the paramount lessons is the *value* of diversity in leadership styles. While the attributes often ascribed to female leaders—such as emotional intelligence, empathy, and collaboration—bring unique strengths to an organization, so too do the typically male-associated traits like confidence and assertiveness. The best leaders understand and embody a range of these qualities, adapting their leadership style to the needs of their team and the demands of the situation.

2. **Self-Awareness Enhances Leadership**: The act of self-rating on leadership attributes highlights the importance of self-awareness in personal development. By understanding one's strengths and weaknesses, a leader can work on areas that need improvement and leverage their strongest attributes. This level of self-awareness is essential for growth and effective leadership.

3. **Stereotypes Should be Challenged**: It's critical to challenge the stereotypes that often box in female and male leaders. Recognizing that leadership attributes are not gender-specific frees individuals from the constraints of societal expectations and allows for a more inclusive and dynamic approach to leading.

4. **Cultural Evolution in Organizations**: This chapter emphasizes the ongoing need for corporate cultures to evolve, promoting equity and inclusion. This evolution includes acknowledging that leadership potential and success are not gender-dependent but rather based on a broad spectrum of attributes that can be found in any individual.

5. **Mentorship Beyond Gender**: In seeking mentors, the focus should be on their expertise and accomplishments rather than gender. This approach encourages a merit-based system where abilities and experiences are valued over any preconceived notions related to gender roles.

6. **Inclusivity and Respect are Fundamental**: The key takeaway here is that dismantling stereotypes and promoting environments of inclusivity and respect is not just a moral imperative but also a strategic one. Such environments are conducive to better performance, innovation, and employee satisfaction.

7. **Adaptability and Leadership**: It is essential to understand the importance of adaptability in leadership. Whether it's adapting to different roles within an organization or to changing circumstances, flexibility is a key attribute that allows leaders to navigate challenges and seize opportunities effectively.

8. **Balanced Leadership for Effective Guidance**: Finally, effective leadership requires a balance of attributes. It's not just about being strong in one area but having a holistic approach that combines different qualities to inspire and guide teams. Leaders must assess which attributes to bring forward in different scenarios, striving to cultivate a balanced leadership style that resonates with diverse team members.

These lessons underscore that while some attributes may be traditionally viewed as masculine or feminine, they are not exclusive to one gender. The best leaders are those who can harness and balance a spectrum of attributes to inspire and guide their teams effectively. By internalizing these lessons, individuals can develop a more holistic understanding of leadership, foster inclusive workplaces, and enhance their leadership capabilities, regardless of gender.

REFLECTIONS

"A woman is like a tea bag – you never know how strong she is until she gets in hot water."

Eleanor Roosevelt

CHAPTER SEVENTEEN

Forgiveness and the Power of Positive Influence

Kimrey Tefft, CEO of True Team

A t the time of my interview with Kimrey, I had known her
for almost three years. We immediately connected and de-
clared ourselves soul sisters; we could have been sisters from another mother. There were several common bonds: we are Southern
belles through and through and even sound alike when we talk.
We both came from broken homes, as did most of the women
interviewed for this book. We both had long and successful careers
in hospitality and are female entrepreneurs with women-owned
businesses.

You do not need to know Kimrey for long to recognize her
incredible drive and energy. When I asked her what fuels that
drive inside her, she told me without hesitation about this remarkable woman who profoundly impacted her life: her mother, Betty
Davis Davis. No, that is not a typo. Miss Betty's last name was
Davis, and she married a Davis. She said, "I was very lucky to be
raised by a mother who set an example of strength and made me
feel like I could do anything. I saw a woman who got up every day,
went to work, and was not only a single mom and sole provider
for the home, but she also made me feel special and loved." Kimrey
remembered her mother's words fondly when she told her she was
moving to New York with Marriott. Her mother said, "I always
wanted you to spread your wings and fly, but not that far!"

The positive affirmations and belief from her mom, combined

with the strength and determination she embodied, produced a strong confidence in her. She said, "With my upbringing and encouragement from my mom, it never crossed my mind to not own my seat at the table."

Kimrey graduated from UNC-Chapel Hill and earned her degree in organizational development. Like her fellow graduates, the roots of home and familial bonds wrapped tightly around her spirit. However, the allure of distant horizons tugged at her soul. With the flame of wanderlust illuminating her path, she applied to join the ranks of American Airlines and Marriott International. During her first interview with Marriott, there was a genuine connection with the recruiter, Emma Davis. Mrs. Emma, as Kimrey calls her, was a woman in her 70s filled with joy and wisdom. She said to Kimrey during the interview, "I believe in you. I see something special in you." That heartfelt interaction was the spark that started Kimrey's 20-year career in hospitality.

At 22 years old, as a new graduate, Kimrey accepted her first job as a human resources specialist at a hotel starting at $6.00 per hour. Working in the human resources department, she realized quickly that Marriott encouraged a promote-from-within environment and supported associates with training to cross disciplines and the ability to move up in the organization.

Her first boss was Meg Bobinski, the director of human resources and operations for the Marriott in Raleigh, North Carolina. Meg was an unselfish leader who taught her all the fundamental skills required in her discipline. "Meg was in the position I dreamed of having, and she tactically set me on a path to get there. That training was foundational to everything I did professionally for the next 20 years."

When the final interview day came, Kimrey showed up looking very professional in an ivory-colored pantsuit but had no idea that Marriott's dress code did not allow women to wear pants. As part of the interview process, she had to meet with the general manager, whose office was near the sales office. Following her interview, the sales team, primarily women, went into his office to protest the "no pants rule." They expressed how professional Kimrey looked in her pantsuit and had been offered the job! One of the first assignments given to her was to rewrite the dress code for that hotel, for the first time ever allowing women to wear pants to work. The requirement was that the pants and the coordinating jacket were bought as a suit and not separately. Unfortunately, the hosiery requirement took many more years to be eliminated.

Sandra LeBlanc was another strong female mentor in Kimrey's career. Sandy gave Kimrey her first director of human resources position in Williamsburg, VA. This was Sandy's first general manager role, and she had become the company's first black female general manager. It was in this position, at 25 years old, that Kimrey witnessed her first taste of discrimination toward females in the workplace. In the first executive meeting she attended, other members were asking why and how Sandy had gotten the job and whether she was qualified or if race played a role. Then came the whispers in the hall about the company's youngest director of human resources, like, "I wonder who she slept with to get that job?" Hearing such discriminatory comments from executives was new for Kimrey, and she was shocked. She had never been exposed to this type of bias. It didn't slow down either of them; she said, "Sandy and I went on to achieve some of the highest results in the company at that location."

The single most impactful mentor that Kimrey spoke of over the course of her career was Vicki Stille. Vicki was the leader who, from the moment they met, demonstrated the skills and attributes that she wanted to possess. Kimrey said, "She was who I wanted to be when I grew up. She modeled the way for me in every aspect of life. She worked hard, loved hard, and became one of the best friends I have ever had. On my first business trip with her, she switched our plane tickets on the jet bridge, gave me her first-class seat, and took my ticket to sit at the back of the plane. I was shocked. It wasn't just a seat change. She thought I was *worthy* of sitting in first class.

Me? First class? It had never crossed my mind as a possibility." It changed everything, including how she would treat people for the rest of her life. Kimrey went on to say, "That moment changed everything for me. Since that day, I wanted to make everyone I encountered feel like they were first class, too. It was an incredible feeling, and I wanted to pass it on to others any chance that I got."

Many years into her career, she would once again work with Sandy LeBlanc. The Southern-born and bred country girl was off to the big city of Philadelphia. Little did she know that God was putting her in the right place at the right time. She was about to face a tragedy that would have a lasting impact on her life. God was placing her where she would be surrounded by the right support group when she needed it most. The team she went to help would be the team that helped her.

If you do not think life can change on a dime, this story proves it can. Kimrey was in her new position in Philadelphia for less than a month on a one-year assignment when tragedy struck her family, completely altering the course of her life. This was one of those make-or-break-your-life moments. The people who are around you in those moments matter.

Since I did not feel I could capture the depth of the bond created with her team in Philadelphia during one of the most difficult situations in her life, I asked Kimrey to write her account of this beautiful story of support, resilience, and healing:

Sandy and My Philly Crew – *The Marriott Philadelphia Downtown, where 95% of my staff had the most challenging upbringings, surrounded by crime, poverty, and broken homes. I was one of three Caucasian members on a team of close to 100 in just one department. Some of them claimed that the new uniforms I ordered for them were the nicest outfits in their closets. They wore them out to nightclubs after work, feeling so proud of how they looked in them. During my first week, I conducted one-on-ones with all of them and asked them what I could do for them. One very special member of the*

team exclaimed to me, "You're going to be my ticket out of the ghetto!"
I was so eager to make a difference in their lives. They made it clear
to me that they had never been shown love and appreciation at work
before. I knew I could give them that in spades.

Little did I know that a month into the job, my baby brother,
Ian, at the young age of 18, would be senselessly murdered in the
very neighborhood where I grew up. There had never been any crime
there. People didn't lock their doors or their cars. The unthinkable
had happened, and I was devastated. After three months of grief
and intense trauma therapy, I returned to work. I was met with
more love, open arms, and stories of understanding than I could
have ever imagined. You see, almost everyone on the team there had
experienced something similar in their own lives. Some of them had
lost family members in the streets of Philadelphia at young ages;
some happened right in front of their homes.

The unlikeliest group of people, the ones I believed I was sent to
mentor and serve, were now mentoring and serving me. They nor-
malized my experience because it was typical for them. No one in my
life could have ever supported me the way that they did because my
family and friends back home could barely process what happened
themselves. I felt included there, safe there, and supported there like
nowhere else.

In the face of adversity, some of the deepest friendships are
often developed. While it had only been one month, it might have
seemed inexplicable for this city-center team of hotel employees to
support Kimrey wholeheartedly. Yet, they found a shared understanding in her tragedy. Beyond that, what additionally bonded
them was Kimrey's ability to step into her leadership role with
empathy, genuinely meeting them where they were. She showed
them compassion and made them not just feel like they mattered –
they came to *believe* that they mattered. Amid this tragedy, a bond
was created based on both parties' needs that would last a lifetime.

At the time of Ian's death, Kimrey had been newly married for just four weeks. While the marriage did not survive the aftermath of the tragedy and untimely murder, the bond she created with the associates of the Marriott Philadelphia survived. She continues to be in contact with those individuals today. It is a positive example of how people from different backgrounds can find lifelong friendships despite the perceived division in some of our communities today.

When asked how she became a female entrepreneur, she laughed and said, "I never wanted to be one! I still don't." She explained that the drive and courage to start her company was a pull from inside her that couldn't be ignored. As she had climbed the corporate ladder, she found it to be rather lonely at the top. The higher you go, there seems to be a lack of confidants who would not only have skills that could help you grow, but also the willingness to generously help you be more successful while not judging you if you asked for help. She saw a need for a company that provided "a confidential, experienced partner" for business leaders. She said, "I just want to be in the background whispering in their ear what I have learned and what I know works. I want to see these leaders get where they need to go and help them save time and money on the journey."

Twelve years later, Kimrey still invests in her own personal development and training. She continually hones her skills as a facilitator, always striving to become more effective. Her desire to stay relevant in team building and coaching has contributed significantly to the success of her company, True Team.

I asked Kimrey to provide some advice to the leaders reading this book who have an entrepreneurial spirit and a vision of owning their own business. She immediately said, "Run, don't walk, pick up the phone, message someone doing what you want to do. Call more than one person. Find the top five people who are successful at what you want to do and talk to them. Don't think they will not take your call or they are too busy. They will be happy to give back what they have learned."

The biggest fear most people have when stepping into their own company is leaving the systems behind. Systems protect people. Leveraging technology is not everyone's skill; organization and procedure may suffer without technology. It can be lonely starting a business, but there is power in networking and mentorship. The devil's in the details of a successful business's legal and financial requirements. Hire professionals for these areas if that is not your scope of work or expertise.

Kimrey is the first to say she benefitted significantly from mentorship. Her career is a solid example of how quickly you can grow and succeed, whether in a large corporate environment or in business for yourself, when you have the right people to coach and advocate for you. Concluding the interview, I asked her to share her thoughts on mentorship.

I asked her, "What would you say to someone considering coaching or seeking a mentor?"

"Sometimes, as adults, we pride ourselves on being independent. We want to achieve success on our own. Maybe we believe that's the only way. Perhaps we didn't have any mentors growing up, so we mistakenly believe we won't have any in adulthood. We often struggle in silence and take longer to achieve our goals because we don't want to ask for help. If it's not offered to us proactively by someone else, we wrongly believe that asking for help or guidance signals incompetence when it actually signals strength."

She continued, "The truth is that most people appreciate being asked for their expertise and advice. They will generously share their experiences and lessons learned with you so that you can avoid or minimize the pitfalls and obstacles that they encounter. When I started my adult life, I was all about being 'Miss Independent.' Boy, did life show me the value of interdependency. I would encounter women from all walks of life who would not only enhance my life, but many of them ultimately saved it."

At this point, I feel Kimrey and her son Ethan need to be invited to my family reunions and holiday celebrations. This is a cookie-cutter example of my personal life growing up and my career path. There are a few other common bonds: we both have a solid faith foundation, and our glass is always full. In the face of adversity, failure, and life doing what life does, we always tend to focus on the positive. She is an inspiration to everyone she encounters! Kimrey touched me deeply the first time she shared the story of her brother's murder. She said, "When I walked into the apartment, it was a crime scene, and my first reaction was to leave because I should not be there, but suddenly it was like this overwhelming feeling came over me, and all I could hear in my mind was, "Forgive them, for they know not what they do.'"

The Bible teaches us that we must forgive others in order to be forgiven, but not many people can truly do that in the worst of circumstances. Her life is a testament to the power of forgiveness. She did not allow the tragedy of her brother's murder to embitter her but chose to rise above it by forgiving the perpetrator.

When I asked her what was next for her, she responded, "I just want to help more people, serve more people, and break the cycle of financial fear that I witnessed my mom live all her life." I am certain Kimrey's mom is correct, believing she can do anything she sets her mind to. I am super excited to watch what the future holds for Kimrey and her company, True Team.

TAKEAWAYS

1. **The Power of Positive Role Models**: Kimrey's mother, Betty Davis Davis, serves as an inspiration for her. Her mother's independence and support instilled in Kimrey a sense of confidence and the belief that she could achieve anything she set her mind to.

2. **The Value of Mentorship**: Kimrey's career was significantly influenced by her mentors, some in positions above her, some beside her, and many who reported to her. Mentorship can provide guidance, support, and opportunities for growth in one's career.

3. **Resilience in the Face of Adversity**: Kimrey's personal tragedies, including the murder of her brother and the subsequent suicide of her father, were profound and unexpected life-changing events. Her ability to return to work and find support and understanding from her team in Philadelphia highlights the importance of resilience in challenging times.

4. **Building Deep Friendships**: Adversity can often lead to the development of deep and meaningful friendships. Kimrey's bond with her team in Philadelphia, despite their different backgrounds, is a testament to the strength of relationships formed during difficult times.

5. **Entrepreneurship as a Response to Unmet Needs**: Kimrey's decision to start her own business, *True Team*, was driven by the frustration of seeing unmet needs in the market. Entrepreneurship can be a response to identifying gaps and finding innovative solutions.

6. **Seeking Guidance and Networking**: Kimrey advises

aspiring entrepreneurs to seek guidance from those who have succeeded in their desired field. Networking and mentorship can be invaluable for learning and growing in a new business venture, and by being proactive in seeking out education and staying informed, one can navigate the complexities of entrepreneurship with greater confidence and strategic acumen.

7. **Embracing Interdependency**: Kimrey emphasizes the value of seeking help and guidance from others. Often, a willingness to ask for assistance can lead to quicker growth and success.

8. **The Power of Forgiveness**: Kimrey's ability to forgive the perpetrator of her brother's murder is a powerful example of the strength of forgiveness in overcoming tragedy and choosing a positive path forward.

These lessons reflect the importance of personal relationships, resilience, and a proactive approach to achieving one's goals and making a positive impact in both personal and professional life.

REFLECTIONS

"When you are grateful, fear disappears, and abundance appears."

Tony Robbins

Chapter Eighteen

Leaders on W.A.T.C.H

A s I wrap up this collection of life and leadership lessons, I want to reiterate how my life and career have been impacted by both men and women alike, and on any given day, one can perform equally or better than the other. What I hope you will take away from this book is that it matters how you show up every day as a leader and a person of influence. The cultural experience of your direct reports within the company you own or represent, regardless of the best intentions for a positive culture, is shaped by your daily interactions and how you treat them.

To whom much is given, much is required. Being in a leadership role comes with a great responsibility. At some point in your career path, it must stop being about managing up and chasing personal gain. You will need to pivot and focus on finding your real purpose, pay it forward, and leave a legacy others will remember. I promise you, the sooner you take that approach, you will find that power will be replaced with favor, and I would choose favor over a power play any day.

When you leave this world, people will not remember your title or how much money you made. They will remember your impact on them in their lives and careers. One of my personal role models is Mother Theresa. My favorite quote from her is, "Not all of us can do great things. But we can do small things with great love."[18]

For many years, my journey from aspirations to achievements was fueled by my own personal gain. "Give me the title and show me the money." Somewhere around the 20-year mark of my career, I realized I was profoundly impacting people. I wasn't just impacting the people who worked with me but also the people who were watching me on my journey.

When I received my first above-property role as a VP of sales and marketing, a press release announced my new position. I started receiving congratulatory notes, and many people would say how I had impacted their life and career. Wow! What a responsibility! I really had no idea how broadly my influence was being felt.

It was an epiphany for me, and it was then that I flipped the script and decided to be more intentional about my impact on the career and lives of others. It was no longer about my personal gain but about others who could benefit from my leadership if I was intentional about how I executed. When I began to focus on the legacy I would leave as a leader, it was a game changer!

Who knew how important this kind of approach to leadership would be as we are currently navigating the aftereffects of a worldwide pandemic? ...What I call the "tsunami after the storm." Today, two open positions are available for every person actively seeking employment. The hospitality industry was hit hard with furloughs and layoffs. Many people chose not to return to the industry.

The people entering the workforce today are no longer solely motivated by titles and money. Their priorities are more centered around work-life balance. Perhaps the next generation is flipping the script to more of a work-to-live approach than a live-to-work mentality. That mindset change may not be a bad thing. Maybe it is a reset that needs to happen. What it does mean is that depending on how long you have been in a leadership role, you may need to also commit to a significant mindset shift.

Are you ready to change your mindset and adjust your leadership style to be more relevant to the men and women entering the workforce today? If your answer is yes, great! I will give you something that will change your leadership style and perhaps your life.

The rest of this chapter comes from a sermon my granddaddy, Rev. A.B. Whittington, preached when I was but a child sitting in his church. Recently, I had the opportunity to hear my daddy, Rev. Jim Whittington, preach the same sermon at a convention in Orlando, Florida. I do not think the timing is a coincidence that I would hear the wisdom of this message again as I am finishing this book. After all, what is a sermon but a life lesson that we ponder and embrace to positively impact our lives? It matters how you treat people, show up for people, and impact the lives of others. You are responsible for at least 50% of every interaction and communication you have with your family, friends, and colleagues. And you are 100% responsible for what you bring to the relationship.

My granddaddy and daddy preached this sermon to win souls to the kingdom of heaven. I share this with you to help you improve your interpersonal skills and leadership game.

As leaders and people, we must always be on W.A.T.C.H., striving for excellence in everything we do. What does that mean? It means we must bring the absolute best version of ourselves every day in every way in every facet in which we interact with others. Leave your troubles at the door; you can always pick up that baggage on your way home.

Let's break it down...

W stands for words

Proverbs 18:21 - The tongue has the power of life and death, and those who love it will eat its fruit.

Your word truly is your bond. Your words should bind without a contract or an agreement. If you tell someone something, they should be able to count on it.

As a leader, there is power in your words. Your communication must be confident, firm, and fair. You also need to consider the listener; people are motivated in different ways, and as the leader, you must adapt your communication style, when possible, to provide the most impactful message for the person listening.

You can destroy someone's confidence or inspire them to greatness with your words. Choose your words carefully. Think before you speak.

There is also a lot of power in the pause or just being silent. I recently saw a sign that said:

Listen and silent have the same letters. Coincidence?

I think not. Silence and pausing before you speak can be an excellent communication skill. When you are silent, the person you are talking to has time to digest what you have said and think about how they can act on what you told or asked them. At times, no words are truly the best choice of words.

A stands for actions

1 John 3:18 - Dear children let us not love with words or speech but with actions and in truth.

Actions speak louder than words. Grandmother Whittington used to say, "Your actions speak so loudly I cannot hear what you are saying."

The way you carry yourself speaks for you even before your words do. Your first impression is essential; people see you before they hear you.

Once you reach a certain level, you must be aware that people are watching everything you do. They watch how you carry yourself and how you interact with others. They look for clues as to how you live your personal life. I was recently reacquainted with a person who worked in a hotel I oversaw ten years prior, and she told me her grandchildren called her Gigi because that was what my granddaughters call me. That blew me away. I did not even know she knew that. But she was watching and listening when I did not even realize it.

Strive for excellence in your life and career. Perfectionism is not attainable, but excellence is.

T stands for thoughts

Philippians 4:8 - Finally, brothers and sisters, whatever is true, whatever is noble, whatever is right, whatever is pure, whatever is lovely, whatever is admirable – if anything is excellent or praiseworthy – think about such things.

Granddaddy would say, "A bird may land on your head, but you do not have to let him build a nest." So, the lesson is that you cannot always control the thoughts that come into your head, but you don't have to allow them to take root and live there.

Before you show up for the people who depend on your guidance and leadership, you must ensure your thoughts promote positive psychology for you personally. The thoughts or voices in your head determine your confidence level and your mood. Don't create a toxic environment for your team by showing up frustrated and complaining daily. Work your own thoughts out before you enter the stage of leading others.

As you now know, I practice a life of "I am" meditation. When I read *Wishes Fulfilled* by Dr. Wayne Dyer, it changed my life by changing my speech. Two of the most used words in speech are "I am."[19]

I am good. I am hungry. I am leaving. I am tired. I am blessed. I am hurt. I am successful.

The basis of Dr. Dyer's book comes from the story of God speaking to Moses in the Bible. God said to Moses, "I AM WHO I AM. This is what you are to say to the Israelites: 'I AM has sent me to you.'" Exodus 3:14.

Dr. Dyer teaches that whatever you put behind the words "I

am," you are putting them out into the universe to exist. As you go through the rest of your week, be mindful of how many times the word that comes behind "I am" is either a positive affirmation or a negative one. I have tried to eliminate most negative ones to affirm more positivity in my life.

C stands for company

Proverbs 13:20 - Walk with the wise and become wise, for a companion of fools suffers harm.

It has been said that birds of a feather flock together. My dad says if you want to be successful, you must associate yourself with successful people.

When people hang together, they catch each other's appetite. They begin to like the same things, imitate each other's actions, and dress alike; they will even start to use the same phrases in their speech. Have you ever noticed how hanging out with people who use a lot of profanity will make you begin peppering more profanity into your speech? The people watching you will judge you by the company you keep. Even if it isn't really who you are, their perception of you will be influenced by the people around you.

And while you are watching your company, be that person others seek out and want to be around. People on your team and in the organization will want to follow you and work with you if they believe you are someone who can be a positive influence on them and their careers. Be willing to impart your knowledge and expertise to others.

H is perhaps the most important letter of this lesson.

H stands for heart

Proverbs 4:23 - Above all things, guard your heart, for everything you do flows from it.

Most of the vital organs in our body have a backup. You have two eyes, ears, hands, feet, kidneys, and lungs; the brain has the left and right sides. The heart has no backup; you have but one heart. Take care of it and use it wisely.

When my granddaddy preached this sermon, he would always tell this joke:

One day, the eyes said, "I am tired of working; I am going to quit seeing."
The ears said, "Well, in that case, I am going to stop listening."
The legs chimed in and said, "I am going to stop walking."
The brain said, "If you are all quitting, I am going to stop thinking."
To which the heart said, "If you don't all stop this nonsense and get back to work, I am going to stop beating."

A leader must have heart. Compassion and empathy are very important tools in your toolbox. Remember, you are likely several station stops ahead in your journey in comparison to the people on your team. Lead with compassion, not criticism. Show them grace in their struggles. Coach them to learn from their mistakes; it will build their confidence. Remember, it wasn't that long ago when you were at their stop in your career path, and someone showed you empathy and helped you grow. Please pay it forward.

Companies and people that invest in their associates' continued education build loyalty. To be an excellent coach, teaching, developing, and mentoring are how you will have the most significant impact on those you lead.

As you walk into each day with this incredible gift of leadership on your shoulders, be a leader on W.A.T.C.H.

Watch your words; speak to people how you want to be spoken to. Inspire with your words.

Watch your actions and strive for excellence; people are watching you.

Watch your thoughts; you must first inspire yourself with positive thoughts and flick away the negative ones so that you can be an inspiration to others.

Watch your company; remember, when you hang around someone, you will acquire what they have an appetite for. Choose your acquaintances carefully.

Watch your heart; be kind and show empathy. Meet people where they are.

In the grand scheme of life, there is one thing you cannot control, and that is time. Everyone will have their season in the sun, but one day, the final curtain will come down. When we are young, we never think we will be old. When we are old, we are amazed at how time has gone by so quickly. So, live each day to the fullest. Don't spend time wallowing in self-pity; be resilient. Be kind; it matters how you treat others. Forgive; grudges only hurt the people carrying them. Finally, love unconditionally.

I will leave you with this beautiful poem I have heard my daddy quote many times.

The Clock of Life

The clock of life is wound but once,
And no man has the power
To tell just where the hands will stop
At late or early hour.

To lose one's wealth is sad indeed,
To lose one's health is more,

To lose one's soul is such a loss,
That no man can restore.

The present only is our own,
Live, love, toil with a will,
Place no faith in tomorrow,
For the clock may then be still.

Robert H. Smith

TAKEAWAYS

1. **Leadership Transcends Personal Gain**: The transition from self-focused ambitions to a legacy-oriented mindset is pivotal. Leaders must understand that their actions and decisions shape the culture of their organization. It's crucial to recognize the influence one has over others' careers and lives, and hence, strive to leave a positive and lasting impact.

2. **Leadership is Relational**: The lasting impact of leadership is certainly relational, not transactional. Titles and financial success are fleeting; what endures is the effect you have on individuals. The memories and feelings you create in others through leadership and personal interactions are what will be remembered long after material successes are forgotten.

3. **Awareness of Influence Necessitates Intentional Leadership**: Realizing the extent of your influence should compel you to become more intentional with your interactions. Shifting focus from personal accolades to the development and enrichment of others marks a significant evolution in one's leadership journey.

4. **Adaptability in Leadership Is Key to Relevance**: As societal norms and workforce motivations evolve, so must leadership approaches. The shift towards valuing work-life balance over traditional rewards like titles and compensation requires leaders to reassess and adapt their leadership style to remain effective and influential.

5. **Communication Is a Powerful Leadership Tool**: Words have the power to build or destroy. A leader's speech should be confident and clear but also tailored to

the audience for maximum impact. Equally, silence and the art of listening can be potent tools for effective communication.

6. **W.A.T.C.H. Framework for Leadership**:
W = Words: The significance of thoughtful and impactful communication.
A = Actions: The importance of actions aligning with words, as actions often speak louder.
T = Thoughts: Maintaining a positive mindset to influence others effectively.
C = Company: Associating with the right people to reflect and enhance one's success.
H = Heart: Leading with compassion and empathy to truly connect and develop one's team.

7. **A Leader's Mindset Directs Their Path**: The content of a leader's thoughts is critical. By cultivating a positive internal dialogue, leaders can foster a constructive and encouraging environment for themselves and their teams. This also involves surrounding oneself with positivity and wisdom to reinforce a culture of success.

8. **Empathy and Coaching Are Cornerstones of Impactful Leadership**: A leader's heart, demonstrated through compassion and empathy, is central to their ability to effectively guide and develop their team. Investing in people's growth not only builds loyalty but also creates a nurturing environment where learning and development are paramount.

In summary, this chapter emphasizes that leadership is not just about personal gain but about making a positive impact on others, adapting to changing workforce priorities, and embodying qualities represented by W.A.T.C.H. to be an effective and compassionate leader.

REFLECTIONS

"It is literally true that you can succeed best and quickest by helping others to succeed."

Napoleon Hill

Final Thoughts

In conclusion, it is my hope that you found *Lead Like a Girl* a compelling and empowering book that offers invaluable insights and guidance for female leaders in today's complex and ever-changing world. I hope you felt celebrated, and you were able to realize the unique strengths and perspectives that you bring to leadership. If you have experienced challenges and biases along the way, perhaps you found some tools to help you overcome them. I encourage you to embrace your full leadership potential, break through barriers, and lead with confidence, authenticity, and resilience.

As you have explored the pages of this book, I trust you realized how embracing a leadership style that is informed by empathy, collaboration, and emotional intelligence can be a tremendous asset in the workplace. *Lead Like a Girl* not only challenges traditional leadership norms but also provides a roadmap for navigating the corporate landscape, entrepreneurship, or any leadership position with a fresh and dynamic approach.

The stories of remarkable women leaders, the practical strategies, and the thought-provoking advice found within these pages serve as an inspiration to all leaders, regardless of gender. *Lead Like a Girl* is a call to action, urging us to create a more inclusive, diverse, and equitable world where leadership knows no gender boundaries.

This book is a reminder that the qualities typically associated with leading "like a girl" are, in fact, the qualities that make leaders great. It's an invitation for all leaders, both aspiring and established, to harness their inner strength and embrace their leadership potential. With this book in hand, the future of leadership is indeed looking bright, inclusive, and powerful. *Lead Like a Girl* stands as a testament to the incredible impact leaders have on the people and the teams they lead. It is a resounding call to action for us all to lead with courage, compassion, and conviction while lifting each other up.

On the morning following the submission of the final chapter to my editor, I found myself seeking a special message to conclude this journey. Later that morning, I spoke with my brother, Brandon Whittington, the accomplished owner of BW Builders, a successful home-building company in Wilmington, North Carolina.

We were having a deep conversation about the ability to turn to prayer and seek answers from God. During our conversation, Brandon shared a remarkably impactful insight with me: "I had to stop being a dreamer, and I had to become a doer. When I was dreaming, I was not achieving. When I stopped being a dreamer and became a doer, then my dreams started coming true." His words resonated deeply.

In closing, I implore you to carry this profound statement with you. While knowledge is undeniably crucial for success, it remains futile if not complemented by action. To achieve your aspirations, you must embody the spirit of a doer. The most meticulously devised plans demand execution.

I mentioned to Brandon that a biblical passage exists that mirrors the wisdom he shared. In James 2:17, it is written, *"In the same way, faith by itself, if it is not accompanied by action, is dead."* This timeless verse underscores the undeniable truth that faith and dreams must be accompanied by purposeful action to bring them to life.

As you embark on your leadership journey, remember these words and, like my conversation with Brandon, may they serve as a guiding light, illuminating the path to your dreams and successes as a leader.

Acknowledgments

Two years ago, I was prompted to think about what I would do with the last half of my adult life. I took that challenge very seriously. It was a pivotal moment for me as I began to think about my purpose for the remainder of my life. I recently read a post on social media that resonated with my vision. It stated, "Your purpose is not the thing you do. It is the thing that happens in others when you do what you do." My granddaddy Whittington preached a sermon titled, "Retire is not in the Bible." I accept his teaching as it relates to continuing to help and serve others.

Turning your dreams into a vision is the first step to achieving; executing the goals to make that vision a reality can sometimes be the most challenging part of success. You must recognize you cannot do it alone; you need support from the people in your village. It is important to have people in your life who are willing to make personal sacrifices, perform extra duties, and often take a back seat so you can achieve those goals. I have been incredibly blessed with family, friends, and talented people who were not only willing to make those sacrifices but were also consistently there cheering me on and encouraging me.

Lead Like a Girl would not have been possible without my personal village. Indulge me while I applaud them.......

My husband, Lenny Casiero, for always allowing me the freedom to pursue my dreams. You have never laughed at my aspirations; for more than 35 years, you have been there to celebrate the successes or pick up the pieces of shattered dreams. You have been the stable foundation of our home, and I love you for taking care of all the details of our life. You are my inspiration, my muse.

To my mother, Glenda Gasaway, and my father, Jim Whittington, your love and encouragement made me believe there were no limitations to what I could do. Thank you both for raising me in a Christian home and teaching me the importance of faith and a relationship with God.

To my life coach and sister, Joy Thrash, thank you for teaching me the power of not asking why but asking why not. I may be the oldest sister, but you are the first person I call when I need advice, and you inspire me every day in so many ways. Forgive me for the cliché, but I am not only grateful to call you sister, but also friend.

This project would not be possible without the small but mighty team I assembled when I decided to write this book.

Frances Owen, Editor and Creative Director, you are the brains behind the vision. I love that you strive to figure things out. For every question about self-publishing a book, you researched a solution and kept the process moving. Thank you for not judging me for writing like I talk, but patiently editing every sentence to make me sound smart.

Randi Raphael, Deus Luz Creative Marketing, Marketing Director, thank you for hearing my voice and depicting it so authentically and eloquently.

Chris Buckelew, Rampant Marketing, Webmaster extraordinaire, thank you! You are amazing at your craft. FLC Business Consulting and *Lead Like a Girl* have greatly benefited from your knowledge of digital marketing.

I am so grateful for each of you and blessed beyond measure that you believed in my vision. This project would not have been possible without your incredible talent and contribution. Thank you for all the evenings and weekends sacrificed so my vision could become a reality.

I would also like to acknowledge the amazing women who agreed to share their stories. I am in awe of the determination and resilience each of you holds. Thank you for allowing me and the people who read this book to learn from your trials, successes, and, most of all, leadership experience. I am certain the vulnerability you were willing to share will be some of the best learning moments for the reader.

Lastly, thank you to my Father in Heaven for giving me this amazing life. I am equally grateful for every tribulation and every triumph. You have never failed me in any of the moments of my life, and for everything life has taken away from me, you have given it back in abundance. I give you all the praise!

James 1:2-3: Consider it pure joy, my brothers, and sisters, whenever you face trials of many kinds, because you know that the testing of your faith produces perseverance.

May you always live peacefully, laugh often, and love unconditionally.

About the Author

Lovell Casiero stands as a testament to the rich tapestry of leadership and ministry that spans four generations in her lineage. Born in the southern heartland, she embodies grace, determination, and resilience. As an author, Lovell undertakes the significant task of guiding her readers through a transformative journey of self-evaluation and purpose. Her writing seeks to inspire and provide tools for individuals to approach opportunities in relationships, leadership, and personal well-being with a discerning and strategic approach.

Her professional journey saw her rise from a sales administrator role to the echelons of senior executive positions. However, her path was not linear; she took a ten-year hiatus to spearhead her family's television ministry. Under her stewardship, what began as broadcasts on local stations blossomed into a global presence.

Life has been a relentless teacher for Lovell, with its myriad of ups and downs, but her indomitable spirit shines through in every chapter of her life. It is the belief that favor over power that fuels her captivating spirit and drive. As a senior executive, author, professional life coach, and renowned speaker, Lovell mesmerizes her audience with authentic tales of her life stories, surmounted obstacles, and realized dreams.

Behind her charismatic presence lies a truth that drives her daily: challenges and hardships are futile unless one can turn them into lessons for others.

If the ideas and stories in this book have sparked your interest, and you would like to spread this inspiration to your organization or community, please reach out. We can explore ways I can help by creating custom workshops for teambuilding, and coaching opportunities for your executives and emerging leaders.

Also, if you're planning a keynote for your next conference or event, I'd be thrilled to collaborate in designing a presentation that engages your audience and meets your goals.

For those wishing to share this book more broadly within your network, company, or educational institution, we offer the option of bulk orders. This allows you to disseminate the valuable insights and lessons from these pages among your team or students, encouraging growth and stimulating meaningful discussions.

FLC Business Consulting | Lovell Casiero
lovell@lovellcasiero.com
https://www.linkedin.com/in/lovellcasiero/

I welcome the opportunity to collaborate with you to spread these messages further. Your engagement and support mean the world to me, and I look forward to connecting with you soon.

1. https://www.parentingforbrain.com/formative-years/

2. https://www.politico.com/story/2018/03/31/this-day-in-politics-march-31-1776-491169

3. https://www.archives.gov/historical-docs/19th-amendment#:~:text=Passed%20by%20Congress%20June%204,women%20the%20right%20to%20vote

4. https://www.archives.gov/milestone-documents/voting-rights-act#:~:text=This%20act%20was%20signed%20into,as%20a%20prerequisite%20to%20voting

5. https://www.zenbusiness.com/blog/the-evolution-of-women-in-the-business-world

6. https://www.reuters.com/sports/tennis/us-open-2023-prize-money-how-much-do-winners-get-2023-08-22/#:~:text=WHAT%20IS%20THE%20TOTAL%20PRIZE,prize%20pot%20of%20%2460%20million

7. https://www.history.com/news/billie-jean-king-wins-the-battle-of-the-sexes-40-years-ago

8. https://www.history.com/news/billie-jean-king-equal-pay-for-play

9. https://www.unwomen.org/en/hq-complex-page/covid-19-rebuilding-for-resilience

10. https://musicmayhemmagazine.com/lainey-wilson-reveals-she-auditioned-for-american-idol-seven-times-and-never-made-it-through/

11. https://www.cmt.com/news/nn27j6/lainey-wilson-stuns-w inning-entertainer-of-the-year-and-more-at-57th-cma-awar ds

12. Haley, Nikki | *With All Due Respect: Defending America with Grit and Grace*, published in 2019, St. Martin's Publishing Group

13. https://fortune.com/2023/01/12/fortune-500-companies -ceos-women-10-percent/

14. https://www.jfklibrary.org/asset-viewer/archives/JFKPOF/ 045/JFKPOF-045-001

15. https://www.ncbi.nlm.nih.gov/books/NBK585058/#:~:tex t=Imposter%20syndrome%20(IS)%20is%20a,accomplishme nts%20among%20high%2Dachieving%20individuals

16. https://www.goodreads.com/quotes/1339572-when-the-st udent-is-ready-the-teacher-will-appear-when

17. Dyer, Dr. Wayne W. | *Wishes Fulfilled: Mastering the Art of Manifestation*, published in 2012 (first edition) by Hay House, Inc.

18. https://proverbhunter.com/quote/not-all-of-us-can-do-grea t-things-but-we-can-do-small-things-with-great-love/

19. Dyer, Dr. Wayne W. | *Wishes Fulfilled: Mastering the Art of Manifestation*, published in 2012 (first edition) by Hay House, Inc.